BEYOND CARBON

NIHARIKA KOSANAM

STARDOM BOOKS

www.StardomBooks.com

STARDOM BOOKS, LLC.
112 Bordeaux Ct. Coppel, TX 75019, USA

FIRST EDITION SEPTEMBER 2023

STARDOM BOOKS

A Division of Stardom Alliance
112 Bordeaux Ct., Coppell, TX 75019, USA

www.stardombooks.com

Stardom Books, United States Stardom Books,
India

BEYOND CARBON

Niharika Kosanam

p. 138

cm. 13.5 X 21.5

Category:
BUS072000 BUSINESS & ECONOMY:
Development and Sustainable Development
NAT011000 NATURE:
Environmental Conservation & Protection

ISBN: 978-1-957456-28-7

With Deep Gratitude and Love

This book is dedicated to you, Nanna

Your selflessness has been a constant reminder of the power of unconditional love.

I'm ever grateful for the lessons you taught me, the values you have instilled in me through your actions, and the immeasurable impact you've had on shaping the person I am today. Your wisdom, kindness, and gentle presence have been a source of inspiration, making me believe that anything is possible with perseverance and dedication.

CONTENTS

INTRODUCTION

Change is the only constant across the entire timeline of Earth. We, human beings, are also a result of that change. Had the change never taken place, we would now not exist. If the Earth's timeline were mapped onto a human arm, it would start at the shoulder, when the Earth came into existence approximately 4.6 billion years ago. Animals emerged within the palm, but the plethora of forms extant today blasted onto the scene around the first knuckle; blocks down the fingers indicate the periods that followed, such as the Jurassic and Cenozoic, during which humans formed a minuscule sliver at the tip of a fingernail. 99% of the four billion species that evolved on Earth are Extinct now. Extinctions are a natural process of the Earth's evolutionary process.

All life forms have one essential purpose: survival. Dinosaurs could survive for 165 million years. Humans, being the most intelligent species that ever existed, have accelerated the change to such an extent that there is not enough time to understand the consequences of their doings and the complexity of the results to respond, reverse it, and even avoid the wipeout. We have made it worse by creating new dangers such as nuclear weapons, pollution, deforestation, overpopulation, and destroying balance in the natural ecosystem by eliminating forests.

This brings to my mind the image of a curious toddler, newly discovering the power of their own arms. Excitedly, they throw objects with abandon, eagerly exploring their newfound abilities while occasionally stumbling, running, and inadvertently causing harm to themselves. In a similar vein, as humans settled and their fundamental needs were met, they were presented with a vast world of seemingly limitless resources. With the advent of machines and the industrial revolution, they enthusiastically embarked on a quest to seize everything within their reach. However, after several generations, the realization dawned upon them that their relentless pursuit was causing harm to the very environment that sustains their existence.

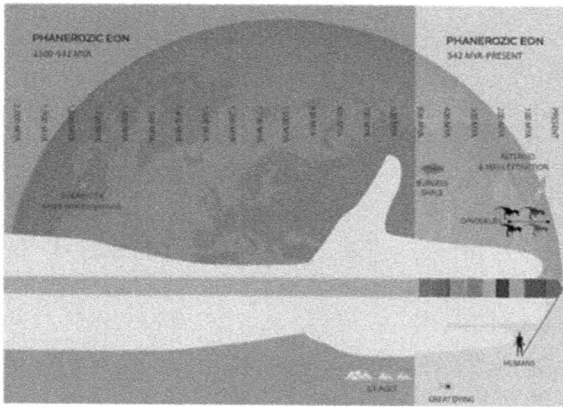

Humans have the intelligence to survive another mass extinction, and we could survive for the next three or three hundred or thousand years, but can we do more than just survive? What are we leaving behind for the next generations? A world characterized by an inhospitable atmosphere, widespread hunger, recurring droughts, frequent catastrophes, and escalating diseases.

Earth doesn't need saving; it will continue to exist and perhaps even flourish without our presence. Life, in its remarkable resilience, will persist, and the imprints we have left on the planet will eventually fade away at a swifter pace than we may anticipate. Nature possesses the remarkable ability to break down everything in due time.

This book aims to shift the reader's perspective from merely "saving the planet" to recognizing that it is, in fact, about "saving ourselves." Within its pages, it unveils pathways for individuals to make a tangible difference in slowing down the tide of climate change through conscious decision-making, altering lifestyles, and cultivating sustainable habits.

In today's global discourse, carbon emissions dominate discussions worldwide. However, for an individual, this topic can often feel distant and difficult to relate to on a personal level. The true essence of this book lies in its ability to break down the complexities of the broader issue, moving beyond the realm of carbon alone. It delves into everyday activities and presents simpler ways for readers to actively reduce their carbon footprint.

The opening chapter aims to provide climate enthusiasts with a fundamental grasp of the scientific principles underlying climate change, and the following chapters delve into actionable steps that can be taken at various levels:

- Individuals: By embracing changes in lifestyle, adopting conscious thinking, and altering consumer habits, individuals can make a significant impact on reducing their carbon footprint.

- Businesses: Through small adjustments in their operations and methodologies, businesses can play a crucial role in reducing their carbon footprint. This book highlights practical strategies and approaches that businesses can implement to contribute to the fight against climate change.

- Policymakers/Governments: By providing frameworks tailored to different sectors, such as manufacturing industries, and investing in resilient infrastructure, policy makers and governments have the power to drive substantial change. This book sheds light on the importance of policy interventions and offers insights into effective measures that can be implemented.

By addressing these three key stakeholders, this book seeks to inspire a collective effort in combating climate change and creating a sustainable future for generations to come.

1
ACCELERATED CLIMATE CHANGE

"We are the first generation to feel the sting of climate change, and
we are the last generation that can do something about it."
– Jay Inslee

A brief look at planet Earth's long and bewildering history reveals
that change is the only constant. Climate change is a term often used
to describe the changes in the Earth's atmosphere, which may cause
changes in the geological, biological, geographical, and chemical
components of the planet's systems. But the problem here is that the
change is happening at an accelerated rate due to the consequences
of our actions.

We have experienced the effects of climate change in our
lifetimes - an increase in floods, droughts, degradation in the quality
of fertile soil rise in epidemics and diseases are some of the many
examples. However, to fully comprehend the impact of human
activity on the climate and to figure out ways in which we can save
our existence, we need to take a closer look at all the factors that can
affect our planet's environment.

It is assumed that climate change refers to only the current
alarming phenomenon of global warming, and its consequences can
be short-sighted. The climate of Earth's atmosphere is constantly

changing, sometimes due to external causes.

Most experts describe the atmosphere as a dynamic fluid, always in motion. This atmosphere is characterized by its physical properties, such as the rate and direction of its movement. These physical properties are, in turn, affected by several factors, such as solar radiation, the position of continents, the chemistry of the atmosphere, ocean currents, vegetation on the planet's surface, and the orientation of the mountain ranges (among other factors). Some of these influential factors change very rapidly.

The distribution of heat inside the ocean, the chemistry of the atmosphere, and surface vegetation can change at very short intervals. On the other hand, the position of continents, location, and height range of mountains change after long intervals of time. Thus, climate change will always be an ongoing process - affected by various physical properties.

Climate Fluctuation can be considered redundant since the climate is inherently dynamic, continuously undergoing change over the course of years, decades, centuries, or even millennia. Some areas have several years of drought, flooding, or other adverse weather conditions. Such decadal climate volatility complicates human activity and planning. Multiyear droughts, for example, can interrupt water supply, cause agricultural failures, and cause economic and social disruption.

We often think about our insignificance in the Earth's lifetime. These climatic changes occur over an extended period. Some of these changes can occur in mere hours, and some might take hundreds of millions of years.

Therefore, as people interested in building a better future for the world, we must understand the complex nature of our planet. The buzzword "climate change" in its present connotations - referring to the alarming rate at which our world is changing and thus deteriorating - can indicate the sudden acceleration in the change process. Once we understand the various factors that affect the Earth's atmosphere, we can comprehend the current acceleration in the rate of change caused by human activities.

What Are Feedbacks?

As discussed above, we know that the Earth's climate can be affected by several factors. Some of these influential factors are external to the surface of the Earth. Other factors could be a part of the Earth's system but external to its atmosphere. However, in the middle, some factors involve interactions between the Earth's atmosphere and its entire system. These interactions are often called "feedbacks" within the planet's system. Currently, the importance of feedback is being researched across all disciplines to understand their contribution to climate change. You must wonder what these feedbacks are and how they affect climate change. Here is a discussion on a few of these natural processes that can affect our environment.

Tectonic Activities

We often neglect the effect of the tectonic movements of the Earth's crust on our climate. These movements can continue to impact Earth's climate even after millions of years. Research has revealed that these tectonic movements have affected continental masses' shape, position, size, and elevation, along with the bathymetry of oceans. These changes in the topography and bathymetry of Earth's systems have led to changes in the circulation of the atmosphere and the oceans.

A study has revealed that the South Asian monsoon system was created because of the uplift in the Tibetan Plateau during the Cenozoic Era. This was because of the changes caused in atmospheric circulation patterns, causing a difference in the climatic characteristics of Asia and other neighboring regions. Tectonic movements can affect the chemistry of our atmosphere. They are known to affect the concentration of carbon dioxide in the atmosphere. This is because, sometimes, tectonic shifts can create volcanic eruptions, leading to the emission of large amounts of carbon dioxide.

A closer look at the history of Earth's atmospheric composition reveals that the degree of volcanic activity near a tectonic plate has influenced the amount of carbon dioxide in the region. Chemical weathering is another phenomenon that can alter the amount of carbon dioxide present on the surface of the Earth. Through a chemical process, a carbon sink can help convert atmospheric carbon dioxide into other inorganic or organic carbon compounds. Tectonic movements can influence the rate at which chemical weathering occurs, causing an increase in the absorption of carbon dioxide. This is also seen in the case of the Tibetan Plateau, where tectonic shifts led to increased chemical weathering and, subsequently, a global cooling period during the Cenozoic Era. Thus, tectonic movements have a significant role in the planet's geography.

Solar Variability

Do you ever wonder if the Sun is changing, just like us? The answer is yes! Since its formation, the Sun is also steadily increasing its luminosity, known as brightness. This phenomenon can significantly affect Earth's climate; hence, we must continuously closely monitor the increase in Sun's luminosity. Sun is a significant energy source, directly responsible for driving atmospheric circulation, and constitutes the biggest supplier of our heat budget.

The Sun being the primary source of energy that drives our climate, it is reasonable to predict that changes in the Sun's energy production would cause the atmosphere to alter.

The radiative energy we receive from the Sun changes at small intervals because of solar storms and other disturbances. Researchers also spend time recording and documenting the variations in solar activities - like the changes in the frequency of sunspots. These variations are recorded from decadal to millennial timescales, sometimes at even longer timescales. However, an analysis of the data we have received regarding the Sun's changes reveals that the amount of solar energy we have received on Earth has been the same since the 1950s.

However, despite this steadiness in the amount of heat we have received, the temperature on Earth has continued to increase. Thus, when discussing "climate change," we observe that the reasons behind the surge in temperature and its consequences are more artificial than natural. Therefore, we must dismiss any doubts that the Sun is responsible for the unprecedented global warming we observe. However, the Sun's energy output can have other forms of impact on our climate. Research has indicated that the decrease in solar activity and the increase in volcanic activity was the main reason behind the Ice Age between 1650 and 1850. This led to the cooling of Greenland and surrounding areas (from 1410 to 1720s) and the advancement of glaciers toward the Alps.

Since 1880, the graph above compares global surface temperature changes (red line) to the Sun's energy received by Earth (yellow line) in watts (units of energy) per square meter. The lighter/thinner lines represent annual values, whereas the heavier/thicker lines represent 11-year average trends. Eleven-year averages decrease the inherent noise in the data from year to year, making the underlying trends more visible.

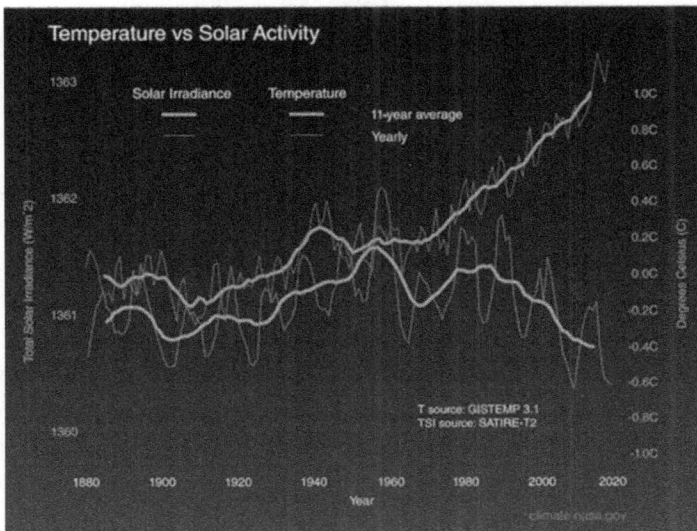

Temperature vs Solar Activity

Since the 1950s, Earth's quantity of solar energy has followed the Sun's regular 11-year cycle of modest ups and downs, with no net increase. Global temperatures have risen significantly throughout the same time. It is safe to conclude that, as a result, it is exceedingly unlikely that the Sun has driven the observed global temperature trend over the last half-century.

Most importantly, if the Sun were to have been the main reason behind global warming, we would have observed warmer temperatures in all layers of our atmosphere. Instead, we can see that the upper parts of the atmosphere are cooling, whereas the middle and lower parts of the atmosphere are getting warmer. This can be associated with increased greenhouse gases, causing more heat to get trapped in the lower atmosphere. Moreover, scientifically speaking, despite an increase in solar heat, there cannot be an increase in temperature as high as we have observed without an increase in the emission of greenhouse gases.

Thus, even when previous Ice Ages are a testament to the impact of varying orbits around the Sun, the rapid increase in temperatures around the surface of the Earth cannot be associated with the Sun alone. The Sun remains an essential source of power for life on Earth, allowing the surface to stay warm enough for all of us to survive. The Sun has several interesting phenomena of its own. We don't realize this, but essentially, the Sun doesn't always shine at the same level of luminosity.

The brightness increases and dims periodically, and it takes 11 years to complete one such solar cycle. During this cycle, one can observe many changes in the activities and appearances of the Sun. Changes in solar energy, the amount of material released into space by the Sun, the sunspots and solar flares, and the size and number thereof are all variations. These fluctuations affect the Earth's surface and climate. However, when the Earth can emit the same amount of energy as it absorbs, the budget remains balanced, causing the average temperature to remain stable. However, ever since the advancement of industrialization in the 19th century, we have observed that there has been a rise of 1°C.

This temperature rise is happening much faster than the fluctuations that are caused due to the Earth's orbit around the Sun. This increases the burden on ecosystems, making it harder for them to adapt to the changes.

Human Activities

In the above sections, we understood how natural phenomena can affect our planet. The striking truth is that despite the enormity of the effects of these external causes, the impact of human activities is the most consequential in the accelerated rate of change on our planet. The above phenomena were to bring to light that we, as humans, have caused damage against all universal odds – altering the Earth's chemistry to an existential limit.

The advent of agricultural modes of production stands as a transformative milestone in human history, shaping societies in profound ways. However, it is essential to acknowledge that the cultivation and consumption of agricultural food have had substantial implications for the climate. These climatic shifts, in turn, have exerted influence on the cultivation and domestication of crop plants, ultimately leading to the domestication and naturalization of animals as well. Thus, the impact of agriculture extends beyond mere sustenance, intertwining the interconnectedness of human civilization, climate dynamics, and the evolution of flora and fauna.

However, it is not agriculture but the rapid industrialization of our planet that has caused a fundamental change in our climate. Increased human activity has led to a rise in global temperatures, melting ice and heating our oceans. This is because of the unprecedented increase in greenhouse gases in our atmosphere. Research has shown that carbon dioxide levels have increased to 405.5 parts per million as of 2017, which continues to rise. This indicated a 41% increase in radiative fencing, causing the warming effect on our planet. The rise in carbon dioxide levels attributes to around 82% of the radiative forcing that has increased in the past ten years.

If human activities and intentions do not change, we may see even more increase in the level of greenhouse gases in our atmosphere. This will lead to an increase of about 3 to 5 °C in global temperatures even before the end of this century.

This stands in direct contradiction to the goals outlined in the Paris Agreement, which was signed by 196 countries at the United Nations Framework Convention on Climate Change. The agreement aimed to limit global warming to a maximum of 2°C and strive for a more ambitious target of 1.5 °C. Despite these objectives, the past two decades have witnessed the warmest temperatures ever recorded in human history. Additionally, there has been a rise in extreme heat events and the establishment of new temperature records at local, regional, national, and global scales. Heatwaves have become more frequent and have shown a tendency to last longer durations.

Greenhouse Effect

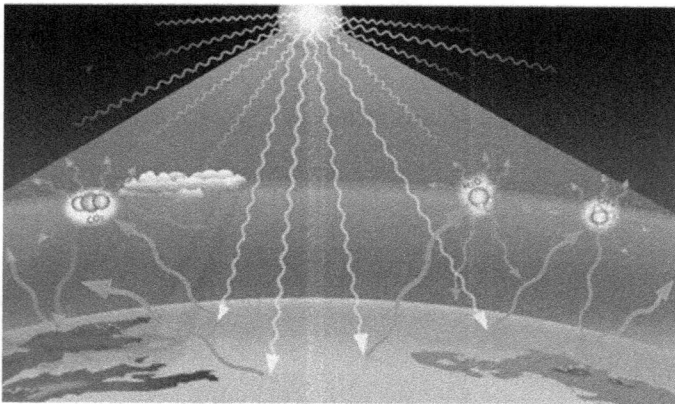

To fully understand the effect of human activity on climate change, we must understand the phenomenon of the greenhouse effect. All analyses indicate that the most compelling reason behind the increase in global temperatures is anthropogenic (artificial). The greenhouse effect is a natural phenomenon here to help us live.

The primary greenhouse gases in the atmosphere are water vapor, carbon dioxide, methane, nitrous oxide, and ozone. The increase in greenhouse gases in the atmosphere creates an envelope that traps heat. This effect helps our atmosphere maintain the optimum temperature for life to thrive.

Due to greenhouse gases, the average temperature of the Earth's surface would be roughly 18°C instead of the present average of 15°C. Many instances in our solar system indicate how crucial having a well-balanced greenhouse effect is for the survival of life on a planet.

Take planet Mars as an example, where the greenhouse effect is insufficient, due to which its atmosphere fails to retain enough heat, leading to a predominantly frozen surface. On the other hand, planets like Venus are entirely composed of carbon dioxide, leading to a hot surface temperature that could even melt. Earth had an optimum greenhouse effect. However, the rise in the emission of greenhouse gases due to increased human activity has led to a dramatic increase in atmospheric temperature.

This increase in atmospheric temperature causes what is popularly known as global warming. Post-industrialization, there has been a tremendous increase in the emissions of greenhouse gases like carbon dioxide, methane, and nitrous oxide. The increase in production and emission of greenhouse gases is also associated with an increase in economic, industrial, and population-related development (observed in humans all around the world). Statistics indicate that the concentration of carbon dioxide has increased by 50%, methane by 150%, and nitrous oxide by 20% since industrialization's advent.

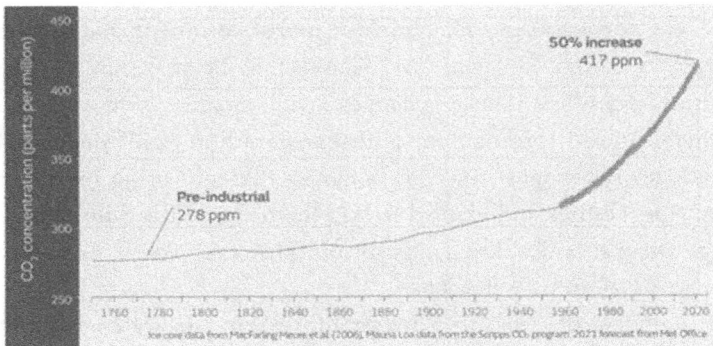

Carbon dioxide levels in the atmosphere have risen from 280 parts per million in 1750 to 419 parts per million in 2021. The last time the atmospheric carbon dioxide content was this high was nearly 3 million years ago. This rise has occurred despite the carbon cycle's natural carbon sinks absorbing more than half of the emissions.

Significance of Carbon Footprint

The term "carbon footprint" has gained significant prominence in recent years. It has become a widely used buzzword adopted by companies and textbooks alike to raise awareness about the environmental degradation our planet is facing.

The concept of a carbon footprint refers to the total amount of greenhouse gas emissions, primarily carbon dioxide, that is generated by an individual, organization, or product throughout its lifecycle. It serves as a measure of the impact of human activities on the climate and the environment.

As per current statistics, the annual carbon footprint of an individual living in the United States is 16 tons. This is an unusually (though not unexpectedly) high carbon footprint compared to the average for the rest of the world, which is 4 tons. As per experts, to preserve what is left of our planet, we must all come together to reduce the carbon footprint of each individual on the Earth to up to 2 tons.

Several corporations, policymakers, and governments have taken strategic decisions to help in making this decrease in carbon footprint possible. These changes will include switching to sustainable food production and consumption and decreased dependency on gadgets for daily activities (like not using the dryer to dry your clothes and instead letting them dry in the Sun). These changes may sound a little insignificant. However, the impact they will have on all of us is immense.

It is impossible to plan a better future for our planet without considering changes at the individual level, as well as at the policy level. For example, taking a flight from one place to another continues to be one of the largest emitting activities we can undertake. At the moment, just a return flight from Los Angeles to London has a higher carbon footprint than the annual carbon footprint of an individual living in Senegal, Africa. Thus, we can consciously decide our travel plans to be more ecologically sensitive. At the same time, governments can look into flight prices and frequencies to prevent overconsumption of our limited resources.

Earth Overshoot Day

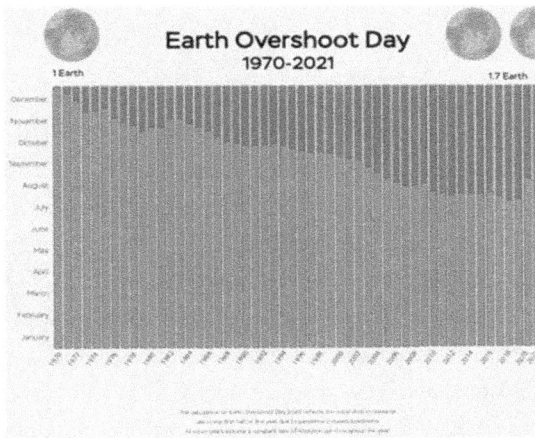

Dec 3 | Indonesia
Dec 6 | Ecuador
Dec 20 | Jamaica

Nov 8 | Colombia
Nov 11 | Egypt
Nov 14 | Guatemala
Nov 24 | Iraq
Nov 25 | Cuba

Feb 10 | Quatar
Feb 14 | Luxembourg

Oct 11 | Uzbekistan
Oct 12 | El Salvador

Mar 13 | Canada, United Arab Emirates,
United States of America
Mar 23 | Australia
Mar 26 | Belgium
Mar 28 | Denmark
Mar 31 | Finland

Apr 2 | Republic of Korea
Apr 3 | Sweden
Apr 8 | Australia
Apr 12 | Czech Republic,
Netherlands, Norway
Apr 18 | Slovenia
Apr 19 | New Zealand, russia
Apr 21 | Ireland
Apr 23 | Saudi Arabia

Sep 3 | Peru, Thailand
Sep 4 | Algeria
Sep 12 | Vietnam

May 4 | Germoney, Israel
May 6 | Japan
May 7 | Portugal
May 11 | France
May 12 | Spain
May 13 | Switzerland
May 15 | Bahamas, Chile, Italy
May 17 | Montenegro
May 19 | United Kingdom
May 21 | Greece
May 29 | Croatia
May 30 | Hungary

Aug 12 | Brazil
Aug 19 | Namibia
Aug 25 | Costa Rica
Aug 27 | Ukraine
Aug 30 | Venezuela
Aug 31 | Mexico

Jul 5 | Bolivia
Jul 8 | Paraguay
Jul 17 | Panama

Jun 1 | South Africa
Jun 2 | China
Jun 11 | Romania
Jun 22 | Turkey
Jun 24 | Argentina
Jun 27 | Iran

Scientists have devoted their lives to figuring out not just climate-friendly solutions but also ways in which we can make the world more aware of the threat of global warming. For many of us, this inevitable future seems distant and incapable of affecting us. However, the truth is that many nations, especially underdeveloped and developing countries, are already facing the brunt of climate change. Earth overshoot day is one concept that has played a significant role in presenting the daunting arrival of climate change in our lives. The theory derives from the fact that at the current rate of consumption of our planet's resources, we would need 1.75 Earths to sustain the same level of consumption. This concept has brought to light the ecological deficit, also known as a global environmental overshoot. It has been observed that humanity has been in an ecological overshoot since the 1970s.

This future has been depicted in the popular Amazon Prime show 'The Expanse' based on the novels by James Corey. Earth Overshoot Day is when we have consumed more resources than we can regenerate in the year. Earth Overshoot Day was in late September 2000 and on July 29, 2021. We have crossed the mid-way and are closer to depleting all our resources.

All statistics indicate that our annual demand exceeds Earth's biocapacity and ability to replenish its resources. As per the National Footprint and Biocapacity Accounts, it has been reiterated several times that at the rate at which we are consuming, we will need 1.75 Earths to sustain ourselves. This has led many young conspiracy theorists to imagine a future where we colonize other planets like Mars and even the Moon to support ourselves.

The illustration below depicts the biocapacity per person of all the world countries. It is visible that most of the planet's resources are being consumed by a select few nations, whereas the others are being exploited despite lower ecological footprints.

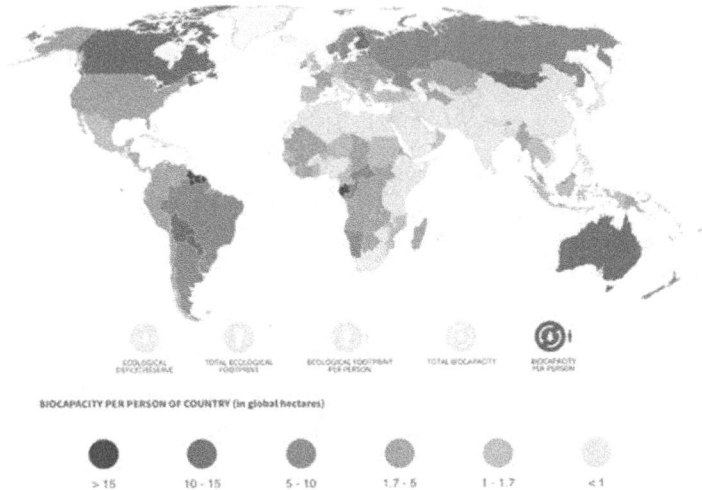

BIOCAPACITY PER PERSON OF COUNTRY (in global hectares)

| > 15 | 10 - 15 | 5 - 10 | 1.7 - 5 | 1 - 1.7 | < 1 |

Biocapacity per person equals the total biocapacity of a region divided by the region's population. For the entire world, the average biocapacity per person is 1.7 global hectares. Countries with an average biocapacity of 3.4 global hectares per person have twice as many resources as the world average. Take the example of India, if you will. We have a biocapacity of 0.4 per person (total biocapacity of a region divided by the region's population).

On the other hand, the ecological footprint of every individual in India is 1.2. Thus, a quick mathematical solution indicates India has a biocapacity reserve deficit of -0.8. These statistics are reported in global hectares as they calculate biocapacity, continuous supply, and ecological footprint, which refers to constant demand.

Furthermore, another alarming illustration reveals more information about ecological inequality in the world. If we were to compare our lifestyles based on nationalities, it would be apparent that climate change is more affected by a handful of countries than the rest of the world. If all of us, every individual on this planet, start living like the people of the United States of America, we would need 5.1 Earths to meet our consumption standards. Similarly, if we were to live like the people of Australia or Japan, we would need 4.5 and 2.9 Earth, respectively.

How many Earths would we need

U.S.A	5.1	
Australia	4.5	
Russia	3.4	
Germany	3.0	
Japan	2.9	
Portugal	2.9	
France	2.8	
Spain	2.8	
Switzerland	2.8	
Italy	2.7	
UK	2.6	
China	2.4	
Brazil	1.6	
India	0.8	
World	1.75	

If we were all to live like the people of India, as per its current average national footprint and biocapacity accounts, we would need 0.8 Earths to survive. As a result, it is evident that India, as a developing country, utilizes far fewer resources than the United States of America and other European nations

Thus, we must consider the political ramifications of climate change. All our conversations on climate change and the steps we need to take to undo these changes have their own social, political, and economic context that we cannot forget. In a country like India, the consumers of fast fashion, fast food, and ecologically heavy practices like flight travel remain a tiny minority of the current population. A huge majority of the nation is economically deprived and also a victim of age-old discriminatory practices of casteism, communalism, and classicism.

Effects on Ocean Systems

Approximately 90% of the heat on our planet is trapped in our oceans, and we even have a system to measure this, known as the Ocean Heat Content. Recent records reveal that the oceans have been getting warmer every year.

Except the eastern equatorial Pacific Ocean, all oceans experienced marine heat waves. In addition to the increase in ocean temperatures, climate change also affects the quality of life. Oceans absorb around 23% of the greenhouse gases (majorly carbon dioxide) released into the atmosphere. This has caused ocean water to become more acidic, harming ocean life in extraordinary proportions. The current pH of oceans is the lowest it has ever been in the past 26,000 years!

Extreme Weather Events

Several regions of the world experienced drastic changes in their weather. In Northern America, very high temperatures (up to 49 °C) were observed during June and July. Cizre in Turkey established a national record of the highest temperature ever at 49.1°C, whereas Georgia also reported 40.6°C in Tbilisi, the highest their temperature has ever been. Heat waves were also observed in the Mediterranean region, with Sicily, Tunisia, Madrid, and Montoro observing a record-breaking rise in temperatures.

Extreme weather occurrences and economic crises have become more common worldwide. Their frequency and intensity have increased, causing many people to lose jobs and lower their quality of life. The consequences of the COVID-19 pandemic have only augmented the perils of climate change worldwide.

As per records, in 2020, there was a peak of undernourishment in the world, with around 768 million undernourished people. In 2021, the world saw a steep increase in global hunger, where reportedly 161 million worldwide suffered from food crises. About 584,000 people faced starvation because of loss of livelihood in

Ethiopia, Yemen, Madagascar, and South Sudan.

Few Quick Facts:

- About 45% of the total carbon dioxide emissions of the world are because of the production of electricity and heat.
- The concentration of carbon dioxide in the Earth's atmosphere is now higher than at any point in the past 800,000 years.
- The wealthiest 10% of the world is responsible for about 50% of the total emissions.
- About 20% of the total greenhouse gases are emitted from industries directly from unregulated human activities.
- Melting ice caps: Since the 1970s, the Arctic has lost about 40% of its summer sea ice volume. Additionally, Antarctica has lost over 3 trillion tons of ice between 1992 and 2017.
- It is estimated that deforestation is responsible for about 10-15% of global greenhouse gas emissions.
- 1/3rd of all the grain that is produced in the world is used to feed livestock.
- Wastage of food is responsible for 6% of all global greenhouse gas emissions.
- By 2011, we had already deforested more than half of the forests in the world to create new farming land.
- For 400 months consecutively, the planet's temperature has been higher than in the previous century.

In short, one cannot emphasize enough that the world is nowhere near where it needs to be to bring down the global rise in temperature.

What Happens If We Are Unable to Stop the Rising Temperature?

According to the Paris Agreement (signed by 196 parties of the UNFCCC in 2016), global temperatures must be reduced to

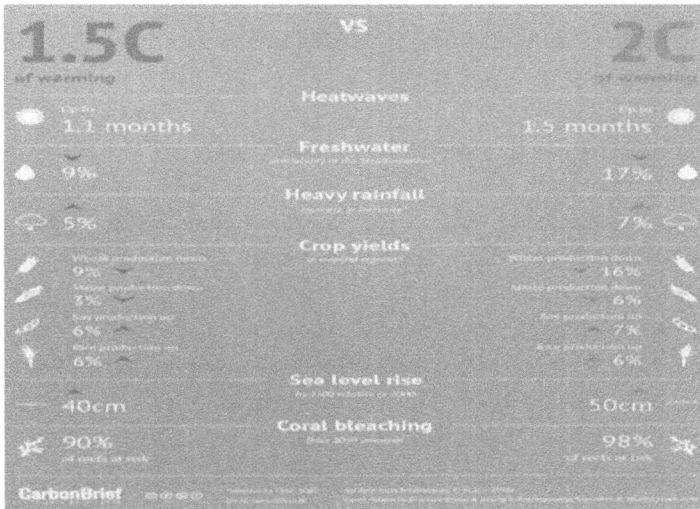

1- 1.5 °C from the expected rise of 4 °C. This increase is compared to what global temperatures were like before the industrialization of the planet. It is important to observe that despite the many environmental reasons behind climate change, human activity remains the largest (if not the only) contributor to the accelerated rise in global temperatures.

The consequences of not preventing this accelerated change shall be alarming. Heat waves in the tropics can persist for up to three months with 2°C warming, compared to two months with 1.5°C warming. According to the agreement: "The additional 0.5°C increase in global-mean temperature marks the difference between events at the upper limit of present-day natural variability and a new climate regime, particularly in tropical regions."

High northern latitudes are predicted to see some of the most significant increases in heavy rainfall, with the maximum during five days increasing by 7% for 2°C warming, compared to 5% for 1.5°C warming. At the same time, the lack of drinking water in the Mediterranean is anticipated to be twice as severe at 2 °C than at 1.5°C, with climate-induced shortfalls of 17% vs. 9% (relative to

1986-2005 levels). According to the study, the global sea level will rise 50 cm by 2100 with 2 °C of warming, compared to 40cm with 1.5 °C of warming (both relative to 2000). Warming of 2 °C will also put 98% of the world's reefs at risk of coral bleaching by 2050, compared to 90% at 1.5 °C.

What If This 4°C Increase Is Not Avoided?

A 4°C increase is similar to the temperature difference experienced as the Earth transitioned from the ice age when large portions of central Europe and the United States were covered by thick ice. Now, you can grasp the magnitude and potential of a 4°C rise in perspective. However, there is a significant difference between then and now. The ice age unfolded over thousands of years, allowing for gradual adaptation and adjustment to the changing climate. In contrast, the impact of climate change caused by industrialization has been observed in just a century. Furthermore, the current destruction caused by climate change is entirely human-induced, while the ice age resulted from natural external factors.

At the current rate of climate change, a global temperature increase of 4°C is projected. Such a significant rise would have dire consequences, including unprecedented heatwaves, droughts, and floods in various regions. These extreme weather events would inflict severe damage upon ecosystems and human systems on an extensive scale.

Here are some potential impacts:

- More Extreme Weather Events: The frequency and intensity of heatwaves, droughts, hurricanes, and heavy rainfall events would increase. This would result in more widespread and severe damage to infrastructure, agriculture, and ecosystems.

- Sea-Level Rise: The melting of polar ice caps and glaciers would accelerate, leading to significant sea-level rise. Coastal cities and low-lying areas would be at greater risk of flooding and coastal erosion, displacing millions of people and causing the loss of valuable coastal habitats.

- Ecosystem Disruption: Many ecosystems, including coral reefs, forests, and biodiversity hotspots, would face significant disruption and loss. Species would struggle to adapt to rapidly changing conditions, leading to widespread extinction and reduced ecosystem services.

- Food and Water Security: Agriculture and food production would be severely impacted by changes in rainfall patterns, increased pests and diseases, and extreme weather events. This could lead to food shortages, increased food prices, and heightened competition for water resources.

- Human Health Risks: Rising temperatures would increase the prevalence of heat-related illnesses and deaths. The spread of vector-borne diseases like malaria and dengue fever may also expand as the habitats of disease-carrying organisms shift.

- Economic Consequences: The economic costs of climate change would be substantial. Damage to infrastructure, increased healthcare expenses, declining agricultural productivity, and the need for adaptation and mitigation measures would strain economies globally.

- Social and Political Instability: The combination of resource scarcity, population displacement, and increased competition for basic necessities could lead to social unrest, conflicts, and political instability in affected regions.

Final Thoughts

To truly comprehend climate change, it is essential to delve into its underlying causes. Through scientific and social investigations, it has become evident that both external and internal factors contribute to the Earth's changing climate. Disturbingly, certain causes have a far more significant impact than others on our rapidly evolving environment. This accelerated pace of climate change can largely be attributed to the increasing influence of human activities.

A closer examination of these human activities reveals the presence of various social and economic factors that contribute to the ecological inequality prevalent in our world. It is imperative to scrutinize the role of developed nations in climate change, as their actions play a crucial role in shaping the future of our planet. Failure to take immediate action would result in the citizens of developing and underdeveloped nations bearing the brunt of the consequences.

In accordance with the Paris Agreement of 2016, it is imperative for countries worldwide to unite and strive to limit the global temperature rise to 1-1.5 °C. However, instead of witnessing a decline in climate change, we are witnessing a rise in global consumption and waste, with no foreseeable indications of slowing down. Urgent action is necessary to address this pressing issue and work towards sustainable solutions that can safeguard our future on the planet.

2
LIFESTYLE CHANGE

"We have forgotten how to be good guests and walk lightly on the Earth as its other creatures do."

— Barbara Ward

An Individual's efforts are as important as the collective efforts of a society, organization, or country as a whole because the Individual's choice drives the entire economy. So, what we as individuals choose becomes the most important & driving factor in accelerating or decelerating climate change. We have observed many changes across generations, with lifestyle change being the most prominent and noticeable.

Let's fact-check for a moment. How frequently have you worn the same gown? You undoubtedly turned heads at the wedding function, received numerous compliments, and then, once all the celebrations were over, the dress found its place in your closet, awaiting its next outing. Does this scenario sound impolite or irrational? Indeed, because you intended to wear it again for an office party. As months go by, you catch sight of the latest trend of wearing sarees with a belt. Consequently, you leave that designer gown untouched in your closet and opt for a trendy saree to wear to the office party. Meanwhile, that pristine kanjivaram saree and the dress you only wore once patiently wait for you to make use of them while you find yourself entangled in the allure of upcoming trends.

The undying urge to keep up with trends is slowly eroding our collective well-being. Throughout the years, consumerism has taken on a new dimension, driving all of us to relentlessly pursue the latest fads and acquire possessions from every possible source. This issue isn't limited to any individual; it affects everyone. In a world abundant with choices at every turn, we have blissfully disregarded the notion of reusing what we already have. If these words seem implausible, one only needs to open their wardrobe and take stock of the sheer number of clothes accumulated, contrasted against how many have actually been worn. It wouldn't be far-fetched to assume that half of that tightly packed closet consists of garments worn a maximum of three times while the other half remains untouched or has seen the light of day merely once.

However, why should anyone be concerned about the number of dresses one purchases? They have worked diligently to attain such purchasing power, and it is not for others to criticize. Shouldn't they have the right to make their own choices? The undeniable truth, however, is that all those garments worn only a few times have already fallen out of fashion. Considering this, they may have already invested a significant amount of money in rejuvenating their wardrobe and could easily dispose of the old clothes as waste. Wouldn't that be reasonable? Can we draw a connection between their consumption rate and the production of waste here? It is evident that the more they consume, the more waste they generate.

Erich Fromm once said, "We consumers are eternal sucklings, crying for the bottle."

In the fundamental structure of any economy, consumers play a pivotal role in the cycle of demand and supply. In earlier centuries, market analysis was conducted to understand the needs of consumers. Based on the demand, production would take place, and the products would be supplied to the end consumers. However, the present scenario is quite different. Nowadays, it seems companies themselves are focused on generating demand in the market. Products are introduced to the market first, enticing customers, and soon a new wave of orders is created. Whether it is the apparel industry or the mobile industry, the pattern remains the same. The manufacturing sector is undoubtedly driven by a mission to continuously augment our needs with each passing day.

In the relentless pursuit of profit-making, society has fallen victim to its own desires. People find joy in their purchasing power and take pride in staying up-to-date, often overlooking the environmental damage caused by their actions. Due to our excessive consumption, we now live in a society where islands of wealth are scattered, yet we fail to recognize the ripple effect this has on the deteriorating climate. The consequences of climate change extend far beyond global warming alone; they resonate loudly in the mounting waste produced year after year. Startling statistics reveal that approximately 33% of greenhouse gas emissions result from direct and indirect waste management. Instead of solely relying on breakthroughs in waste management technology, perhaps it is time to consider individual-level actions and make a difference.

Learning from Previous Generations

Every business house is built to make money. How can we commoners stop them from bringing something new to the market? Of course, we can! Consumers are the king and shall always be. We can play an important role in combating the deplorable state of waste and its management. If we are the creator of this waste problem, it is up to us to find a solution. And for that, we need not wander about or knock at others' doors. The key lies in our age-old tradition and is ingrained in our genes. Let us go back two generations to understand how they lived & how much waste they generated. If we observe how one's parents & grandparents lived, they always used less, wasted less, reused, and upcycled. From storing milk packets to sell, exchanging old sarees for steel utensils, storing & exchanging small metal items for snacks & candies, etc., recycling and reusing existed in every household. There was significantly less waste sent to dump yards.

Can you recall witnessing your father or grandfather engaging in repairs rather than discarding items? It was common to see fathers meticulously fixing the radio, iron boxes, doors, and anything that broke. Nothing was considered disposable. Instead, items were reused for alternative purposes after their initial use.

For example, plastic bottles used for packaging tea powder were reused to store staples. Every Indian household still has the habit of keeping plastic bags and covers for reusing them. It seems easier to curse the previous generation for having caused drastic climate changes. But if we observe closely, the older generation valued every resource and was way more sustainable than we are today. My father never had more than two pairs of footwear at any time, I have five pairs to match for every occasion, and my daughter has 10. The reason still hovers around our changed mindset. People purchase things in their capacity to bring comfort to themselves and their loved ones.

In the present circumstances, it has become commonplace for parents to forego waiting for their children's genuine needs. Instead, they scroll through endless pages on platforms like Amazon or Flipkart, impulsively placing orders for the latest items in the market. Whether it's a dollhouse, a teddy bear, or a craft book, little consideration is given as to whether the purchase is truly necessary. We are drawn to whatever captures our attention without considering factors such as durability, recyclability, or the product's lifespan. The concept of reusing items is absent from our lives, and we fail to pass it on to the next generation. If we closely examine the upbringing of the previous generation, we will find that most individuals did not indulge in such excessive consumption. They embraced the values of preserving products, saving money, and, in turn, safeguarding nature. Why can we not follow their footprint instead of leaving our carbon footprint on Earth?

The present time is witnessing an unnatural behavior of consumption which is undoubtedly unsustainable for our planet. It seems a whole bunch of influential people who have been trying to normalize these unsustainable habits only fill their own pockets. Considering it, one can assume that none of us can have a problem with people running business houses.

However, we must realize that the problem doesn't stop with our consumption. The bigger problem lies in the domain of climate change, where the waste seems to cross all the limits.

A whole bastion of people advocates sustainable living by introducing a minimalistic approach. None of us is alien to this concept because we were witness to the minimalistic lives of our forefathers. The drape of sustainability is not new but has been lost somewhere in our pursuit to acquire every luxury of life. We must acknowledge that our forefathers were more understanding than we are and that our future generations are not supposed to bear the brunt of climate change. If we wish to leave a safe Earth for the generations yet to come, it is high time we chalk out our role in combating the plight of climate change.

A Lifestyle of Fast Fashion

"Over-consumption is cancer eating away at our spiritual vitals. It distances us from the great masses of broken, bleeding humanity. It converts us into materialists. We become less able to ask the moral questions."

– Richard J. Foster

Why do we consume beyond our actual needs? It is essentially the most critical question when we know that consumers are the drivers of every economy. So, are we trying to boost the economy intentionally? That's not the case. The fact is that we are all trapped in the illusion of being better off than the other person in the vicinity.

As humans, we possess an inherent sense of competitiveness. We are constantly observing what others possess, and if their possessions appear more appealing, we strive to acquire the same. We harbor an insatiable appetite for possessing items that surpass those of others. Often, we overlook the necessity of these items and purchase them simply because we have the means to do so. Consider, for instance, a family of two individuals owning two cars or a young school-going child owning a mobile phone. It begs the question: Do these acquisitions truly align with practical needs?

We have embraced a lifestyle that prioritizes showcasing our standard of living. It has become customary for parents of the new generation to compensate for their lack of quality time by showering their children with material possessions. We have mistakenly associated sustainability with sacrifice, yet we are unwilling to compromise on any of our desires. Don't we strive to keep up with our peers by owning the same brand of mobile phone or laptop? Don't we compare our sense of style to that of well-known celebrities? Undoubtedly, we all do. Over the years, we all have been so fond of matching the trend that we have unchained a whole new domain of business called Fast Fashion.

A few decades ago, shopping was regarded as a task reserved for special occasions such as birthdays, anniversaries, or festivals. During that time, consumers would save their money to purchase new clothes only at specific times of the year. But why? Was it because they lacked the means to buy more frequently? Not necessarily. It was primarily because the fashion industry's trendsetters would unveil new designs during particular seasons. However, a shift occurred in the 1990s when shopping transformed into a form of entertainment. A new trend emerged, leading to the widespread production of inexpensive, fashionable imitations. These knock-off garments were affordable, allowing consumers to experience the joy of wearing something similar to what fashionistas donned.

The fast-fashion market has chalked out a clever plan in the supply chain management among fashion retailers. The ultimate goal is to quickly produce affordable clothing in response to or in anticipation of changing consumer demands. Now, consumer demand changes at the bat of an eyelid. It has been assumed that consumers want to adopt every new fashion at a lower cost.

Similarly, the working principle of Fast Fashion seems horrifying when the idea is to make the current fashion trend vanish quickly. Although the façade of Fast Fashion mirrors a beneficial relationship between the manufacturer and the consumers, the reality is far from the idea of sustainability. Fast fashion indeed sounds cool as the clothing and accessories move from the designer sketchpad to the store in the shortest possible time.

However, the question lingers - What is the need for such a concept?

What was wrong with our traditional industry practice? The production cost of Fast fashion merchandise is less; thus, these items always remain within the consumer's budget. The daunting doubt, however, hovers around durability. These garments are not meant to last long and are intended to cash in on a trend, be worn a few times, and then discarded to capitalize on the next new trend.

Nevertheless, it is worth pondering - do we truly require such a concept? What was amiss with our conventional industry practices? The production cost of Fast fashion merchandise is less, and thus, these products always remain within the consumer's budget. The daunting doubt, however, hovers around durability. These garments are not meant to last long and are intended to cash in on a trend, be worn a few times, and then discarded to capitalize on the next new trend.

Have you ever come across the term "microfibers"? It may seem insignificant in the grand scheme of things, but these minuscule fibers have the potential to cause significant disruptions in our vast world. Microfibers refer to tiny particles of plastic found in fabrics made from nylon and polyester. Every time we launder these fabrics, countless microfibers are released into the water, posing a threat to aquatic life. However, we are not immune to the consequences. Microfibers serve as a source of plastic in the food chain. Startling research from the University of Newcastle, Australia, suggests that the average person consumes approximately 5 grams of plastic daily through water consumption. We don't knowingly chew on plastic bottles or other objects, but the microfibers discarded by various industries find their way into the aquatic food chain. As a result, when we consume fish or seafood, we unwittingly consume plastic. These microfibers enter our bodies and disrupt the gut biome, consequently impacting our immune system. The ramifications of microfiber pollution extend beyond the environment and directly affect our own well-being.

In 2019, the size of the Fast Fashion market was $35.8 billion, projected to reach $38.21 billion in 2023. The fast-fashion labels like H&M or Zara produce about 52 micro-seasons a year, which means one new collection of clothes a week which is again meant to be worn immediately, instead of months later. In contrast to the Fast Fashion industry, the traditional clothing industry model operates seasonally. For example, the fall fashion week displays styles for the upcoming spring or summer, and the spring fashion week showcases looks for the following fall or winter. And then, there are often pre-fall and pre-spring fashion weeks or resort collections that take the stage.

According to 'UnEarthed,' the ethical consumer and Greenpeace's journal, if the demand for fast fashion continues to grow at the current atrocious rate, the total carbon footprint of our clothing will reach 26% by 2050. Still wondering how?

It needs a lot of energy to produce, manufacture and transport millions of garments. Most fast fashion industries have set their manufacturing units in countries like China, India, and Bangladesh, which are (almost) entirely dependent on coal for generating power. Similarly, animals like sheep are raised for their wool, and they overgraze the pastures. Overgrazing leads to soil erosion, land degradation, loss of valuable plant species, food shortages, and famine. Cotton processing involves certain chemicals that degrade the soil, while wood-based fibers, like rayon and viscose, cause mass deforestation. Every year, hundreds of thousands of hectares of endangered and old rainforests are cut down, only to be replaced by plantations of trees used to create wood-based fabrics. The collective impact of various factors contributes to the detriment of the Earth's climate.

Fast fashion is indeed a boon for business. The constant introduction of new products makes customers increasingly attracted to stores. Moreover, they purchase the more recent products when they can afford them. That spins the wheel for more production, and the vicious cycle keeps running. Make-Buy-Dispose. If you look closely at those retailers, you will never find your one-month-old dress hanging in their shop window because the retailer never adds to its prevailing stock—instead, it replaces items with newer versions. This strategy instigates over-consumption. We know the current stock will not remain in the market after a couple of weeks. So, we end up grabbing everything available now. Since the clothing is cheap (and cheaply made), it allures people back to the stores, making the art of shopping a daily need, and that is the most dangerous illusion created by the Fast Fashion market.

The fashion industry produces 80 billion garments annually. Since the 1990s, as shopping has become more of an entertainment experience and the need for "fashionable" garments has grown, fast fashion has increased. Fashion shows routinely set the stage for new trends, which can change monthly or even weekly, as opposed to traditional seasonal trends. What's wrong with fast fashion is that it has significantly increased waste in the fashion business.

Several people believe that many significant brands must change their business models to counteract the harmful consequences of rapid fashion. Clothes can travel multiple times worldwide before reaching their final destination, resulting in carbon dioxide emissions, clothing waste, and other pollution issues. Consumers have the option of reducing the adverse effects of quick fashion. Two ways of doing so are buying less clothing and increasing the life of your current apparel. Another option is to go thrift shopping, which reduces the number of products in the trash while also allowing you to buy items at highly affordable prices. Finally, customers can study products before purchasing them to ensure that they are sourced and manufactured sustainably. Ultimately, it all boils down to consumers caring about the adverse effects of rapid fashion and making a conscious effort to alter it. Purchasing long-lasting items rather than cheap ones reduces the demand for virgin materials. We indeed need clothes, and that sustainability advocate is not stopping you from purchasing new clothes. However, we are at such a critical stage of waste creation that our unsustainable consumption has come under scrutiny. As a consumer, we often feel blessed to have encountered this concept of Fast Fashion, for it has enabled us to get the clothes we want when we want them. The alluring factor is the affordability and availability of innovative, imaginative, and stylish clothing. Sporting the latest look, being well-dressed, or having a large wardrobe is no longer the province of wealthy people. Fast fashion has put the newest styling into the lap of the commoner. This democratizing influence of fashion has, in turn, made us indulge in fun or impractical items, and now everyone wears something different every day. As days pass by and new things start ruling the market, we all dump the old ones and grab the new ones. The result is nothing but the increasing burden of waste on the surface of our planet. Being insatiable consumers of fashion, are we not responsible for causing these drastic changes in the world?

> "Fast Fashion is like fast food. After the sugar rush, it just leaves a bad taste in your mouth."
>
> – Livia Firth.

Consumers Are the Culprit

The prevailing climate crisis has mutated the famous saying which calls consumers the king. The uncontrolled consumption mode has become a craze in every segment of our life. We buy technology just to show off; our food habits have taken a new avatar; we are crazy about the latest fashions and invariably have become the ringleader of climate change.

The disposal cycle has become more sinister as fashion trends accelerate with a gradual price drop. The major problem in the Fast Fashion industry is that the products are neither recycled nor donated. The waste either goes to landfills or is incinerated. Fast fashion has a devastating environmental impact in myriad ways – Water usage, Microfibers, and Greenhouse gas emission during production and disposal. The indirect effects include deforestation and releasing of hazardous chemicals into the environment. Moreover, the situation is grim considering the human rights violation of laborers in the Fast Fashion industry.

Over-compensation is another lifestyle aspect that is entering urban experiences. Many of us might have observed that parents have become much more lenient with their kids, willing to spend extravagantly to meet their needs and want. This phenomenon is believed to be the result of "guilt." Many parents, caregivers, friends, and even partners feel guilty for not being able to spend time with their loved ones. Giving them expensive gifts has become a common practice, an entirely new and acceptable mode of communication among the wealthy.

The emotional connotations behind these practices have made it impossible to critique them. Who would want to point out errors in these little acts of love in a world which is growing apathetic? However, from the climate change perspective, encouraging these practices is more harmful than ever.

Our vision as a consumer is myopic because we are not shown the reality behind this mad-paced economy. The more we dig deeper into the system, the harsher the reality. Our economic mobility has also increased our appetite for consumption. Today, aesthetic sensibilities play a significant role in the products we purchase and choose to keep in our lives. The availability of many products has made it possible for all of us to use products that meet our individual preferences rather than the need to save resources to save money or the planet.

One of the major byproducts of the fast-fashion textile industry is untreated toxic wastewater. Do we know that textile waste contains substances like lead, mercury, and arsenic that are incredibly harmful to aquatic and human life? None of those stylish dresses come with statistics of waste generated during production. The wastewater from clothes factories is dumped directly into rivers.

Bangladesh, the hub of fast fashion production units, produces 22,000 tons of toxic waste that goes straight into the waterways annually. The contaminated water endangers the health of the wildlife and people who live along the banks. It finally makes its way into the sea and pollutes it.

A huge reason behind the cultivation of the practice is peer pressure from our friends, colleagues, neighbors, and other world participants. We are a conforming species; hence, most of us go out of our way to resemble the person next to us so that we do not stand out and get called names. This attitude has kept many commercial industries afloat, making them insanely successful in today's world. Fashion, mobiles, video games, cosmetics, and even books - the consumption of these products has overwhelmingly become more about setting and following trends.

These brands have shifted from catering to a person's specific needs (with their regional and social identity in mind) to catering to the needs of "target audiences." The term reveals that most of the things we consume daily were never necessarily meant for us. However, we do wish to participate in society. Some of us like to wear a good dress on a dinner date, and others want to consume delicious wine when we can.

So, is it all about waste released during the production process? No. The situation is forbidding the runaway production process as well. One ton of fabric can require up to 200 tons of fresh water to dye and finish. Extinction Rebellion and the UN have confirmed that 3.6 billion people are simultaneously at risk of water scarcity. Just pause and ponder. You are buying a ton of fabric for yourself. But many like you will keep buying until someone tells them about the problem. When a consumer keeps buying, the demand increases in the market and the producers jump in to fill it. The production cycle continues, and resources are exploited irrevocably to satiate the need. So, will this vicious cycle come to an end if you alone stop being the consumer?

Indeed, a significant change can occur through consistent small efforts. When you alter your perspective and adopt a more sustainable approach, you become a positive influence for others to recognize that life can be fulfilling without excessive consumption. By embracing a mindset of mindful consumption, you demonstrate that it is possible to live a fulfilling life while being mindful of our impact on the environment. Your actions inspire others to reconsider their own habits and realize that a more balanced and sustainable approach to life can lead to a sense of normalcy and contentment.

Food Habits

The way we consume food has a similar story as fast fashion spins out. Our current food system is fueling climate change in an unaccountable manner. The world's most extensive product line is the food system, which starts by growing and harvesting crops, followed by processing food. Times have changed, and there is a lot of technological intervention. Every technology uses power which invariably causes greenhouse gas emissions.

Moreover, in the recent decade, we have switched to a trend of acquiring some exotic foods which are not locally grown.

Transporting and marketing those make an impact on the carbon footprint. The agriculture and food processing sectors that sustain 7.8 billion people emit 21-37% of all greenhouse gases annually.

Our food system happens to be as polluting as sectors that generate electricity and heat and produce 25% of greenhouse gases. It is, in fact, more polluting than transportation which contributes to 14% of emissions. Every stage in a food system is directly or indirectly responsible for carbon emissions. For instance, chopping down forests to make way for farms and pastures removes a significant carbon sink and thus indirectly contributes to the emission load in the atmosphere. More often, farm machinery is run on fossil fuels. Manufacturing of agrochemicals and fertilizers has toxic effects on the environment too. Even cattle burps release methane, a far more potent greenhouse gas than carbon dioxide.

However, can we stop eating when the onus is put on our food plates? Unfortunately, unlike other emission-intensive sectors where cleaner and viable alternatives are available to acquire low-carbon energy, the food industry is trapped in a dilemma. Yes, electricity can be sourced from photovoltaic systems instead of fossil fuels, and electric vehicles can be promoted; however, those are all indirect channels. We must understand that carbon emissions are integral to the biological system, and one can never stop eating.

On the same note, we can plan a healthy, sustainable diet and produce within planetary boundaries. At an individual level, we must discourage the over-consumption of food that impacts biodiversity, the environment, and human health. An inclination to favor plant-based diets against meat-based diets is a win-win situation for the Earth and us. These days, our eating pattern has branched out peculiarly. With companies like Zomato and Swiggy, we can order eatables at our doorstep. Consider a scenario where you have already cooked dinner. But then, all of a sudden, the whole family wishes to have pizza, and you place an order. Even if we leave aside the problems caused by the production process, the distance traveled by the delivery partner impacts the carbon footprint.

Moreover, the food you have already cooked either goes inside the fridge or enters the dustbin. We, at our level, may not do anything for the massive chain of processes involved in food production. But we can make significant changes if we consume sensibly and reduce food waste. Similarly, we can reduce the food miles by consuming locally grown foods. In the past, our ancestors did not rely on specific foods like avocados to manage their weight; instead, they maintained a healthy body mass index (BMI) through a holistic and healthy lifestyle. This was aligned with nature's inherent principles. For instance, if mangoes thrived in India, it indicated that the local climate and demographic conditions were suitable for the fruit. However, as we generate increasing demand for exotic foods, we contribute to the concept of "food miles," which refers to the distance that food travels from its source to consumers. This not only impacts the environment but also adds to the overall carbon footprint associated with food production and transportation.

Better To Put a Full Stop

While reading through a sustainability article, you often take a break to connect the dots. A sustainable lifestyle sounds familiar to us, and still, we are so comfortable with our consumeristic attitude that we do not wish to change. But it is high time we change the ongoing trend to set an example for the next generation. It is high time we put a full stop to over-consumption.

Every human bears the same basic need in a world with an ever growing population. One's over-consumption leads to the other's malnourishment. Climate change is a global phenomenon. Furthermore, any change in one corner of the world has a drastic effect on the other side. Our consumption of food, technology, fashion, and everything has a broader impact than we ever see. We, humans, are on the Earth to sustain as a species, but not at the cost of others. Our present way of living reflects a misguided attitude. We live as if there is another planet we can move to once the Earth's resources are over. Remember, there is no planet B. We must renovate the present Earth by incorporating a sustainable lifestyle at an individual level. Are you still doubting your abilities to bring about a change? Look at your children; they are the future generation on this planet. They learn from you. They will surely follow if you abandon the over-consumption and adopt a minimalistic lifestyle.

And as Christine Lagarde once said, "Unless we take action on climate change, future generations will be roasted, toasted, fried, and grilled." We consume at our whim and not based on our needs, and this whim of consuming more and more has carved a comfortable niche in our minds. We MUST change it, not only for us but for the future generation, for the other species on this planet.

How to Beat the Cynicism?

Are you worried about the cynical turn that our conversation around sustainable living is taking? Well, there are so many unique ways in which you can do your bit to control global warming. The world's attitude towards environmental protection and preservation is changing by the day; more and more people are joining the movement toward shifting to more sustainable alternatives.

Over the years, Minimalism has become a popular buzzword on the internet. Whether it be lifestyle bloggers, YouTubers, or big companies, the shift from maximalism to Minimalism has begun. This way of life ensures that we do not fall into patterns of toxic consumerism, a habit where we consume products we don't need.

Minimalism offers a unique experience where you do not have to become a saint and renounce all worldly pleasures; however, you can choose to live a slow life, where these experiences are infrequent and thus extremely special. Over the years, theorists and artists have expanded the purpose of minimalist thought. Minimalism has become a whole way of life - a common theme across different aspects, such as fashion, architecture, make-up, food, etc. Thus, as an individual, you can overcome the decision-making problem by opting for fewer things in your life, enjoying them to their fullest rather than letting them become just another piece on the shelf.

We no longer must depend upon popular aesthetic choices and conform with the majority. We can be our hype squad and find products that are tailor-made for us. It is not uncommon to see a consumer purchase a local brand with stylized personal options like name engraving and customization of ingredients used.

Unlike elite brands with a select few products in their collection, each of which is more obscure than the other, these local brands are better capable of meeting the standards of every consumer. A cynical attitude that wishes to ignore the perils of the present will do no good. We must identify the pressure points of our current ways of being and eliminate them from our lives.

The immediate satisfaction of fast food and fast fashion has created a cycle of environmental negligence. A change in the perspective of the customers will inevitably change the outlook of the producers and the sellers as well. Moreover, we must take a keen look at our past and cherish a way of life that believes in longevity and creativity.

Plastic Problem or Attitude Problem?

Plastic, once considered a miracle material because of its flexibility, versatility, lightweight, and long-lasting quality, is now creating havoc. We depend on it by including it in garbage bags, credit cards, headphones, etc. Scientists estimate that more plastic will be in oceans than fish by 2050.

What exactly is the problem: Plastic or our 'use and throw' attitude toward plastic? Here is the time taken for the following items to decompose.

- Plastic bottles: 70-450 years
- Plastic bag: 500-1000 years
- Tin can: 50 years
- Napkins & diapers: 500-800 years
- Glass bottles: 1,000,000 years
- Aluminum can: 200 years

A glass bottle takes million years to decompose. But why glass isn't a problem because we don't throw glass more often. Think about it.

Interesting Studies

A 2014 study for the Progressive Bag Alliance, representing the plastic bag manufacturing and recycling business in the United States, compared supermarket bags made of polyethylene (HDPE), biodegradable plastic, and paper with 30% recycled fibers. It was discovered that the HDPE bags consumed less fuel and water and produced fewer greenhouse gas emissions, acid rain emissions, and solid waste than the other two. The study, which did not include litter, was peer-reviewed by Michael Overcash, a professor of chemical engineering at North Carolina State University at the time. Because of the different carrying capacities of plastic and paper bags, the study employed 1,000 paper bags as a baseline and compared their impacts to the consequences of 1,500 plastic bags. Plastic bags used 14.9kg of fossil fuels to manufacture, but paper bags required 23.2 kilograms. Plastic bags generated 7kg of municipal solid trash versus 33.9 kilograms of paper, and greenhouse gas emissions were comparable to 0.04 tons of CO_2 versus 0.08 tons for paper. Paper used 1,004 gallons of fresh water, while plastic bags used 58 gallons. Plastic consumed 763 megajoules of energy, while paper consumed 2,622 megajoules. The plastic bag produced 50.5 grams of sulfur oxides vs. 579 grams for the paper bag and 45.4 grams of nitrogen oxides versus 264 grams for the paper bag. A 2011

U.K. The study evaluated HDPE, LDPE, and non-woven polypropylene, a biopolymer produced from starch polyester, paper, and cotton bags. Global warming potential, resource depletion (such as fossil fuels), acidification, eutrophication, human toxicity, freshwater toxicity, aquatic toxicity, terrestrial toxicity, and smog creation were all identified as consequences. HDPE bags had the lowest environmental impact of the lightweight bags in eight of the nine areas since they were the lightest bag in the category. It is difficult to dispose of plastic bags because they are light and readily blown around. They end up littering sidewalks and trees and washing into the ocean, where they entangle and are eaten by marine life. They are rarely recyclable and can take 20 to 1,000 years to disassemble. Plastics get broken down into small particles over time by the sun and heat, resulting in microplastics less than five millimeters long. These have been found in the bodies and stomachs of marine animals, as well as in water bodies and on beaches worldwide. While these life cycle studies did not consider litter, the globe acknowledges that the omnipresence and persistence of plastic garbage is a major environmental issue.

Regarding bag selection, Steve Cohen, head of the Earth Institute's Research Program on Sustainability Policy and Management, stated that it is difficult to anticipate because they all utilize carbon. It is impossible to say whether plastic, paper, or cotton bags are the best in net energy or carbon. "However, once a product made of fossil fuels, such as a plastic bag, enters the trash stream, it's there forever," he said. "That is the most serious issue with plastic."

A 2005 Scottish study indicated that paper bags performed worse than plastic in terms of water usage, acidification of the atmosphere, and eutrophication of water bodies, which can lead to algae development and oxygen depletion.

According to a Danish study that compared LDPE, polypropylene, bleached and unbleached paper, cotton bags, and a few others, LDPE bags had the lowest environmental impact. Unbleached paper bags were shown to have the same global warming potential as LDPE bags. However, the ecological implications of bleached paper were significantly higher than that of unbleached paper—To save 43 trees, a paper bag would have to be reused 43 times to meet the environmental impact of LDPE.

Paper bags have a higher environmental impact since they are six to ten times heavier than plastic bags, use more fuel, and cost more to carry and distribute. According to one estimate, it would take seven trucks to convey the same number of paper bags as a single truck full of plastic bags. Their mass also consumes more room in warehouses and landfills.

However, the magnitude of the repercussions from paper bags is determined by whether the forest is managed sustainably and the environmental measures utilized in the paper production plant.

Bags designed to endure longer are typically made of heavier materials, requiring more resources to manufacture and thus having a bigger environmental impact. Paper and cotton bags must be reused many times to equal the comparatively low global warming impact of plastic bags; however, neither can survive long enough to be reused sufficiently to equal the lower effect of plastic bags. In the end, using a bag only once is the worst option. Reusing as many bags as possible is the key to lowering your environmental effect.

Thus, an inward look at our choices can reveal our relationship with the environment. Through an overview of these lifestyle decisions, we can attempt to live a green and clean life with minimal effort. The beauty of such a choice is in the joy of learning a new way of life, devoid of societal pressures. What's more, an eco-friendly lifestyle will not only make your and my life easier. It will leave a better planet for our children as well.

Here are the ways that you can make a difference today:

1. Influence Manufacturers to Create More Environmentally Friendly Products

When you buy sustainable products, you are helping the producers who make them. Growing demand for sustainable products provides new incentives for producers to create and market them. By selecting sustainable items, you consciously decide to lessen your environmental imprint.

You may help businesses that value environmental protection by switching to eco-friendly brands. This is reflected in how these brands source, manufacture, and distribute their products. The emerging crop of specialty zero-waste retailers has things that will last and are better for the environment. You will reduce the amount of waste you generate by purchasing sustainably. Waste arises from various sources, ranging from the packaging of commodities to the goods themselves.

2. Choose Durable Products

Buying durable products instead of cheap ones as they long laster reduces the demand for virgin materials. Though all products, durable or not, use the same raw materials but the longer a single effect lasts, the more time the environment has to recover the materials used to make it.

3. Buying Local

One of the essential strategies to reduce food miles is buying locally to help the environment. When you purchase locally, you are purchasing things made in your neighborhood. When you go grocery shopping, many of the goods you buy travel over 1500 kilometers to reach your plate. By reducing these distances, you are lowering the environmental effect of your meals. Local food does not generate big carbon footprints due to international plane flights or long truck excursions. This reduces fuel consumption and air pollution. There is no need for shipping, packing, or refrigerated facilities. Fresher food is available at your local market.

- There is way less packaging involved.
- Buying local helps the local economy.
- You know from where your food comes if you buy it at the market.

- **Accessibility**

Local firms can function in their respective localities. Because their customers are close by, it is simple for them to bring their items. Consider a farmers' market: customers may readily obtain a variety of locally farmed produce without leaving their neighborhood. Shoppers can easily walk or bike to their local market to browse the stalls. On the other hand, more giant supermarkets and department stores are frequently unable to be positioned centrally. Because larger stores require more space, they often relocate out of town. As a result, shoppers must drive to these stores, increasing their fuel use and carbon emissions.

- **Fresh Produce**

Consumers can enjoy fresh and healthful vegetables by purchasing and dining locally. Many local producers take pride in producing organic, hormone-free, pesticide-free products. This is not only advantageous to the consumer, but it is also beneficial to the environment. Keeping dangerous pollutants out of the air, such as pesticides, helps to improve crops and air quality. Furthermore, because the product is fresh and delivered directly from the farm to the table, there is less waste. Many large retailers have high food waste because things spoil before they are purchased. This food waste is reduced on a smaller scale with a more direct farm-to-table approach.

- **Protect Local Land & Preserve Wildlife**

Purchasing from local markets plays a significant role in the preservation of local lands and animals. By choosing to buy locally, you actively support and assist local farmers and producers. As these farms are owned and operated by local individuals, they are less likely to be sold to developers who may drastically alter the property, potentially causing harm to the existing fauna. Moreover, when large corporations acquire such properties, they may implement farming practices that are environmentally unfriendly and detrimental to the ecosystem. Therefore, by prioritizing local purchases, we contribute to the sustainability and well-being of both the local economy and the surrounding environment.

- **Local Workforce**

Buying local supports the local workforce. For example, if you buy your groceries at a local farmers market, you are assisting in the retention of local growers, makers, and farmers. You're also creating opportunities for other local jobs, such as the team in charge of organizing the farmers' market, the team in the cost of setting up the stalls, the team in charge of cleaning up, and so on. These local enterprises with local employees exist because consumers want local goods. These local enterprises might not operate if there is no consumer demand. Many employees would be forced to look for work outside of the town. This would increase traffic congestion and fuel use, increasing the overall carbon footprint.

- **Fewer Emissions**

Eating local equates to fewer food miles, which means less emission from transport vehicles, which includes airplanes, ships, and trucks. It was found that local-grown produce travels about 50 miles to reach the consumer's table half a day from harvest.

According to an Iowa study, the traditional food distribution method consumes 4-17 times more and emits 5-17 times more carbon dioxide than local and regional systems.

4. Make Your Home a Healthier Place

When selecting products for your home, choosing smarter and more sustainable options can create a healthier living environment for your family. Look for items made from organic and natural materials, as these are often free from harmful chemicals and provide a healthier indoor atmosphere. Similarly, opting for products made from recycled materials helps reduce waste and promotes the efficient use of resources.

5. Make Your Home More Energy Efficient

Achieving energy efficiency in your home can be accomplished through the installation of energy-efficient appliances and the adoption of various energy-saving practices. By opting for energy-efficient appliances, such as refrigerators, washing machines, or air conditioners, you can significantly reduce your energy consumption. Additionally, utilizing house fans, employing bright power cords to minimize standby power, utilizing intelligent thermostats for optimized temperature control, and improving home insulation are effective measures that contribute to energy efficiency.

These practices not only help in conserving energy but also lead to reduced energy bills. By using less energy for heating and cooling, you can lower your overall energy consumption and subsequently decrease your monthly expenses. Embracing energy efficiency not only benefits your household but also contributes to a more sustainable and environmentally conscious lifestyle.

6. Shared Transportation

Carpooling is a practical and eco-friendly solution that can be implemented whenever and wherever possible. By sharing rides with others who have similar destinations or joining carpool programs, you can reduce the number of vehicles on the road, leading to decreased traffic congestion and lower carbon emissions.

When it comes to school transportation, opting for school buses or organized transportation services can significantly contribute to reducing traffic and carbon footprint. Instead of individually dropping off and picking up your children from school, utilizing these shared transportation options helps to streamline the commute and reduce the overall number of vehicles on the road.

Carpooling and utilizing school transportation not only benefit the environment by minimizing vehicle emissions but also promote community bonding and cost savings. It's a practical way to make a positive impact while enjoying the convenience of shared travel arrangements.

7. Conscious Buying

Engaging in conscious buying practices and avoiding unnecessary purchases can have a significant impact on reducing waste generation. By being mindful of our consumption patterns and considering the necessity and longevity of the items we purchase, we can minimize the amount of waste that ends up in landfills.

It is crucial to recognize that while the recycling industry offers significant benefits, there are limitations and potential environmental impacts associated with the process. Recycling operations can release toxins into water bodies, the atmosphere, and land if not properly managed.

To minimize our environmental footprint, it is important to adopt a thoughtful approach to waste management. Before discarding something, we should consider if it can be reused. If not, we should then explore if it can be recycled and ensure it is properly sorted into the appropriate recycling stream. This helps maximize the effectiveness of recycling efforts.

In addition to recycling, there are various behaviors we can adopt to enhance efficiency and reduce unnecessary consumption:

- Choosing products with minimal packaging or those that require fewer resources to manufacture.
- Avoiding the use of disposable or single-use items whenever possible.
- Opting for products that are made from recycled materials, are recyclable, repairable, refillable, reusable, or biodegradable.

By prioritizing these practices, we can minimize waste generation, conserve resources, and make a positive impact on the environment. It is essential to make informed choices and actively participate in sustainable consumption habits for a more environmentally conscious future.

8. Set a Great Example

Setting a positive example of living a sustainable lifestyle is crucial for future generations, regardless of whether you are a parent or a grandparent. By adopting sustainable practices in your daily life, you can inspire and educate the younger generation about the importance of environmental stewardship.

3
ROLE OF INDUSTRIES

"The fight against climate change is the defining challenge of our time. It requires courage, innovation, and a collective commitment to change."

It seems unlikely to conceive of a world without industries. Over the years, industries and their products have become omnipresent in our lives. We often forget that thousands of products used daily are produced in a workshop in some or another part of the world.

This rapid growth of industries and industrial products, however, has come with its consequences. Industries have become and continue to remain one of the biggest polluters of the environment and, at the same time, also remain unregulated. The amount of greenhouse gases created in the manufacture or processing of a product is commonly used to calculate an industry's contribution to the increasing rate of climate change. The carbon footprint of an industry is the quantity of CO_2 and other greenhouse gases generated when a product is manufactured. Industrial establishments are growing faster by the minute, and projections suggest they will continue to do so.

By 2025, the global manufacturing industry is expected to reach $15.5 trillion in annual revenues, a sum that is comparable to the global IT sector today. The global manufacturing sector has also weathered major technological shifts, meaning that manufacturing jobs will likely remain a mainstay of the economy for decades to come. But despite its central role in the economy, the manufacturing industry faces significant challenges that have slowed its growth.

Most prominently, firms have begun to explore new ways to create more desirable products. To maintain a leading position in the global economy, the manufacturing industry will need to explore and implement sustainable technologies. However, to do so effectively, they will need to incorporate new work methods beyond simply updating technology.

The Future of the Manufacturing Industry

Many challenges are hurtling towards the manufacturing industry. Climate change, demographic trends, and changing customer needs mean manufacturers must develop new products and services. Yet, creating them will take time, and the manufacturing process will need to be recreated with concepts like design thinking, collaboration, innovative technology, and resharing the economy. Industries need to develop these new products and services quickly and efficiently. The fastest-growing industries in the US, including apparel, furniture, and footwear, are typically not those where you would expect to see significant corporate involvement. Yet through investment and expertise, the companies can secure best-in-class results from these industries. For the manufacturing industry, the issue is not 'which' of the many available technologies will succeed but rather 'how' they will succeed. Issues like labor laws, safety, and wage requirements are those that can ensure success in the long term. At the same time, the industry must evaluate the role of technology in executing ideas. As highlighted in previous chapters, the industry's role in hastening the rate of climate change is enormous. An increase in industrialization has led to increased consumption of goods and services, thus increasing the consumption rate of our natural resources. Therefore, it is evident that the first place where change is required is the industries. Environmental sustainability is integral to an organization's strategy in the modern economy. If your vision is green and environmentally conscious, your business is likely to survive the competitive world.

The manufacturing industry must accept its role in heavy greenhouse gas emissions. In the United States of America alone, industries are responsible for more than 23% of overall carbon dioxide emissions, as per the data released by the Environmental Protection Agency.

Similarly, in Europe, more than 880 million tonnes of carbon dioxide are released annually every year, making it one of the most significant contributors to the increasing greenhouse effect on our planet. Several warnings have been issued about the rising climate change rates. Quite recently, the Intergovernmental Panel on Climate Change also issued a report that indicated the impact of human activities on the rate of climate change. According to the current climate change rate, the world's temperature will increase by 2.7 °Cby the end of this century, bringing hell upon Earth.

Rise of Industries in India

A closer look at countries like India reveals that climate change will have a horrible impact on the lives of the people here. Industry and output are responsible for more than 23% of India's GDP. Thus, we need to control the number of fossil fuels consumed by our endeavors. Climate change is already causing a rise in India's heat waves, droughts, cyclones, and floods. The Energy Policy Institute of the University of Chicago studied more than 55000 industries in India. Their study revealed that there had been an overall reduction of at least 2 % of the generated revenue in industrial plants for every 1 °C rise in the annual temperature of India.

Thus, for India, the direct impact of climate change will be such that the GDP will reduce by 2.5 to 4.5% by 2030! Who would have thought we would be so close to an economic crisis due to the accelerating rate of climate change? In addition to the nationwide economic crisis, data has emerged to show the direct impact of climate change on livelihood. Patterns indicate that global warming will have a more pronounced effect on industries like beverages, wineries, fishing, agro-processing, insurance, and tourism.

Furthermore, according to the Lancet Countdown report on health and climate change, in India alone, climate change will lead to a loss of 118.3 billion work hours and 111.2 work hours per person due to extreme heat - this was the highest for any country in the world.

Pressure on Corporations

The internet has democratized access to data. Previously global corporations had fewer systems of checks and balances. Government regulations and demand for the product were some of the only factors that governed a company's productivity. However, rising awareness of global climate change has made big corporations squirm. Their consumers are demanding change in their products and production values.

The fact remains that today, only a hundred energy corporations worldwide are responsible for 71% of all industrial emissions that have spearheaded human-driven climate change. Additionally, we see an inherent inequality in the causes of global climate change. The top 15 food and beverage companies in the USA are generating more than 630 million metric tons of greenhouse gases yearly. That amount of emissions is more than that of the entire Australian population, which is already among the world's higher emitters.

Thus, it has become important for us to reconsider the production, distribution, and consumption of goods now more than ever. As an entrepreneur, you can keep several things in mind to ensure that your product is ready for an increasingly changing world.

Life Cycle Assessment

There is increased awareness about the unsustainable

consumption levels with which our world is plagued. People are looking at policymakers and businesses with a critical eye, trying to find products that meet the changing standards of the world. It is no secret that companies have hardly ever considered their product's environmental impact.

Many firms have set greenhouse gas reduction targets, but most of such targets fail to account for emissions connected with a company's goods over their whole life cycle. This is significant because when a company manufactures a product, it requires raw materials that release emissions during harvesting, extraction, refining, and other processes known as upstream emissions. When a consumer uses that product, additional emissions result from the product's use and eventual disposal, known as downstream emissions. Failure to account for or mitigate these emissions implies that the great majority of greenhouse gases emitted by corporations are due to them, resulting in little to no waste management on the part of industrial corporations.

Measuring and reporting emissions is the first step, followed by ensuring the accuracy of this measurement and transparent reporting. A "science-based target" must be a target that applies to all of the emissions a corporation's activities and products are creating—not just those emitted while a product is being made in a factory.

A product with a clean and zero-impact life cycle will be able to outperform other products because of its sustainability. Life Cycle Assessment continues to be the most comprehensive method to achieve this new production standard. This process assesses the environmental impact of a product, process, or activity through every stage in its life cycle. This includes extracting raw materials required for the product and the process of production, transportation, usage, and eventually disposal.

Life Cycle Assessment is an integral part of companies today as it helps them determine a product's environmental risks at every stage. This way, they can work on the ecological optimization of the product at every stage, ensuring that the product remains extremely efficient and thoughtful. The assessment also helps consumers know all the important details about the product, helping them make the right choices. Another huge benefit of life cycle assessment is that it creates space for innovation and creative thinking, finding new ways to set your product apart.

What is Life Cycle Assessment?

Life cycle assessment is a term that borrows from the concept of life cycle thinking. As kids, we are introduced to the water cycle, which helps us understand the different stages of water, from its existence as a liquid (water) to gas (water vapor) and then liquid (rain) again (sometimes solid as well, in the form of ice). Today, this information helps us understand the various stages at which our activities can pollute water - in the form of acid rain or oceanic pollution. Similarly, lifecycle assessment is also a method through which we can take a closer look at the components of a product or a service and ensure that it is optimized in every way to suit the needs of the company, consumer, and climate.

Life cycle assessment has become integral to decision-making in government, non-government, and the profit sector. This process involves a thorough analysis of the processes involved in making, distribution, and consumption of a product - this includes the extraction of raw materials, manufacturing facilities, usage purposes,

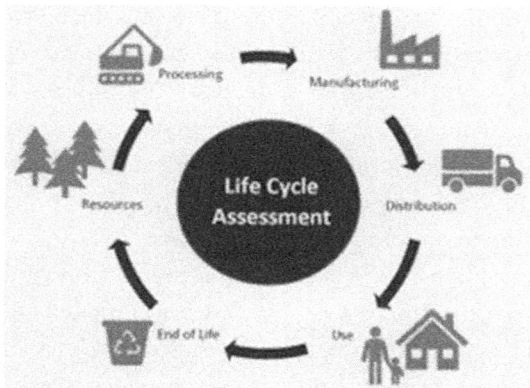

recycling options, and methods, as well as the treatment the product will undergo after the end of its useful life. These days governments, corporates, and individuals are using life cycle assessment to enhance their product design, create and implement better policies, brand through a new degree of benchmarking, and more.

LCA (Life Cycle Assessment) for a company's product will give important input on where the major environmental impacts occur. These major impacts can be either in the supply chain, in the processes owned by the company, or in the use or end-of-life of the product. With this knowledge, a company can formulate its environmental strategy aiming to improve its product's life cycle to reduce the overall impacts associated with the product.

Life Cycle Management (LCM) is closely related to life cycle thinking. The process of LCM involves finding a target, organizing it, analyzing it, and then managing product-related information and activities toward continuous improvement across its life cycle. This will introduce life cycle thinking and product sustainability to all business operations. This is a boon for business owners who strive to reduce their environmental footprints to minimize a business's ecological, social, and economic burdens.

One key characteristic of LCM is for companies to look beyond their operations and downstream and upstream activities outside the company's direct control. If a company is serious about sustainability, it must incorporate new concepts like LCM into its sustainability agenda.

Hot Spot Identification

Hot spot identification refers to identifying essential areas for improvement in a product's life cycle to result in larger natural resource conservation. It is very difficult to evaluate the environmental impact of a product without hot spot identification. This method has also been included and discussed in the National Voluntary Guideline released by the Government of India.

Assessment of life cycles can help companies make more informed decisions. Coca-Cola utilized a type of LCA in 1969 to assess the environmental impact of moving from glass to plastic bottles. Because glass is a natural material, most people expected it to be the more environmentally friendly option. It was later established, however, that utilizing plastic bottles was less detrimental to the environment. Coca-Cola made its decision after examining environmental factors such as energy savings from creating plastic bottles in-house rather than having glass bottles imported. Because glass is heavier, the lighter weight of plastic bottles decreases the energy consumed in shipping. Coca-Cola has begun to employ LCA in India to assess a separate issue. Farmers blamed a Coca-Cola bottling plant in Kala Dera for exacerbating water shortages. The beverage giant consented to an independent third-party assessment in the recently drought-stricken state of Rajasthan, only to discover that it contributed to some of the problems.

Waste Management Inc. is one company that has benefited from long-term thinking (WM). For years, the trash-hauling and landfilling company carried waste from residences to vacant land, a short-sighted method that cost the customer money and degraded the environment. WM established a new business unit to turn "garbage into cash" - with services for businesses to convert previous waste into new raw materials - by applying LCA. One-third of all aluminum produced, for example, is recycled and repurposed. Serving companies like Wal-Mart have transformed WM into a "market maker," transforming methane gas from landfills into new energy sources.

Circular Economy

Our generation saw the rise of disposable alternatives to objects we use every day. The increase in plastic production and consumption is among many commercial factors that have forever altered our lifestyles. For example, we saw an exponential rise in fast food consumption as we no longer needed to go home to prepare a quick lunch. We could go to one of the many outlets for our favorite dishes and pick up food in disposable containers without worrying about cooking, washing, and storing utensils in the middle of the day. However, today we seem to be taking a dramatic U-turn. Environmentalists worldwide are ringing the alarm bells, warning us about the gruesome consequences of non-biodegradable waste. There is a noticeable shift in consumer behavior towards adopting more sustainable practices, and it is heartening to see trends such as carrying metal straws and containers becoming increasingly commonplace. These small but significant changes contribute to reducing plastic consumption and minimizing waste.

Additionally, people are now actively using eco-friendly carry-bags for grocery shopping, which helps reduce the reliance on single-use plastic bags. The growing awareness of the health disadvantages associated with junk food has also prompted individuals to make more conscious choices regarding their diet and nutrition.

This shift in consumer behavior aligns with the concept of a circular economy, where the emphasis is on the principles of "make, use, return" rather than the linear model of "make, use, dispose of."

We also have a design problem apart from the pollution problem. It's time to rethink and redesign how we make and use products. The circular economy directly results from the "make-use-return" concept in businesses, a direct impact of scarcity of resources, growth in population, and climate change. This model is an alternative to the "take-make-dispose of" system that drove the world during the early and Middle Ages of the industrial era. This new circular model aims to create an effective flow of resources, ensuring that the products and materials used to manufacture them are efficient. A circular economy also has the potential to generate significant returns with a triple bottom line. These include economic, environmental, and social benefits like cost savings through improved efficiencies, less material waste, and health impacts on humans and the environment.

In addition to that, a circular economy considers the need to extend the life cycle of a product through various strategies. Remanufacturing is one of the strategies of a circular economy.

Remanufacturing refers to revitalizing used parts of a product through recovery and disassembly. Repairing and recycling are the essential concepts that drive this process.

Design for disassembly is an approach that emphasizes the ease of dismantling and separating products into their individual components or materials for efficient recycling, repair, or reuse. It involves designing products with the intention of minimizing waste and promoting a circular economy.

The concept of Design for Disassembly recognizes that many products are composed of various materials that can have different recycling or disposal requirements. By designing products with disassembly in mind, manufacturers can facilitate the separation of components, making it easier to recycle or repair them to rebuild the same or a different product. This strategy helps combat products with shorter and less effective life spans.

The end goal of businesses today is to make sure they can design products that won't become a part of a dangerous landfill. Part of the global environmental problem is using natural resources at a higher speed than they are reproduced. Design for recycling means more efficient use of energy, natural resources, and raw material, which is a way to minimize local and global environmental problems. Although laws and taxes can enforce recycling, product design is equally important for making recycling as easy as possible. There are three main reasons for recycling:

- Economy - If recycling becomes profitable, no extra driving force is needed, and the market will adjust in a self-regulated process.
- Hazardous materials - It is important to prevent dangerous or toxic materials from spreading in an uncontrolled way in the environment. A legislation will be required to prevent this from happening.
- Preservation of natural resources - If products are recycled, natural resources can be saved using less raw material and less energy. For example, recycled aluminum needs 5% of the

energy needed to produce primary aluminum, and there is also less need for transport, etc.

After a certain point, the product will no longer be able to perform its main function. This does not necessarily mean the end of the life of the product. It could be repaired or used for other functions. At some point, all products will be scrapped, which means disassembling, sorting, reusing, recycling, fragmentation, depositing, etc. The remains of the discarded products, material, parts, or subassemblies will have a significant value if they can be either reused for the original function or downcycled, used for material recycling, or used for energy recovery. Thus, a circular economy thrives on building a business that teaches innovative design and amplifies products that can be reused, repaired, and remanufactured. Through this process, we can safeguard the functional value of raw materials used in making the product and recover the energy they may contain to generate new products.

The new and sustainable business building can also create several new opportunities. The evolution of the circular economy has been

in tandem with the rise of sustainable businesses – leading to an increase in the leasing of resources, better waste management, and reuse of materials. It is believed that the arrival of a circular economy can generate four times more jobs than local business models – helping us build sustainable communities.

End of A Product's Life

Of course, all products reach a point where they can no longer provide the utility they were created and purchased for. However, the mere end of a product's use does not mean that it is not relevant or purposeful anymore. Research has made it easier to repair and reuse the components of a product. Disassembling, sorting, reusing, recycling, fragmentation, and depositing are many ways we can extend a product's life cycle.

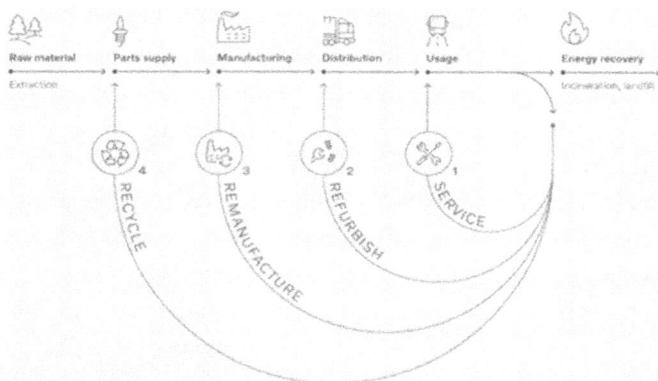

Product recovery is becoming increasingly crucial as we move toward a circular economy. Product recovery management seeks to shut the loop throughout the life cycle of a product. It manages all used and abandoned products, components, and materials to recover as much economic and ecological value as possible while reducing the amount of wasted garbage. Remanufacture, repair, reconditioning, cannibalization, redesign, refurbishing, and recycling are some end-of-life product recovery options. All these end-of-life choices differ, and choosing the best product recovery option should consider various variables. Because of the concept of recycling in the tech industries, systems such as exchanging outdated tech gadgets and items for new ones exist. Mobile phones, for example, are made up of multiple easily replaceable elements. When a specific part breaks, you may replace it yourself rather than dispose of the entire gadget or pay for an expensive repair performed by an expert.

Consider a simple dry iron (cloth iron) that stops working. You decide to attempt the repair yourself. Most products currently require screwing, cutting, and being forced to come apart. You will wind up having a lot of parts but still won't be able to find the problem or repair that one broken piece. But imagine if this iron consisted of only five domains and no fasteners like glue or epoxy were used to hold everything together.

It would make replacing a defective component much easier without replacing the entire product. It would also benefit the environment if people stopped returning entire products because a minor portion was broken and instead began repairing them.

Extended Producer Responsibility

As mentioned earlier, the previous belief of "take-make-dispose of" led to a culture of mass consumption. This reduced the accountability of firms that produce ecologically harmful products, especially those that take no responsibility for the aftermath of the product's consumption. With the recent rise in awareness about global warming, governing bodies have begun to review the idea of extending post-consumption responsibilities to the producers. Extended Producer Responsibility burdens producers with a significant financial and physical responsibility for disposing of products after consumption.

This approach has many added advantages. It can incentivize the need to reduce wastage at all production stages, promote the need to build more sustainable designs, and also popularize sustainability practices for one and all. This policy exists because manufacturers have the greatest control over the design of a product and its subsequent marketing - thus implicating them with the responsibility of taking care of the environmental consequences of the product.

Extended Producer Responsibility can be executed in many ways. Some of them are reusing, recycling, and buyback. Often, producers delegate this responsibility to third parties known as producer responsibility organizations, who are paid to take care of the product's aftermath. This delegation promotes privatization as waste management becomes the responsibility of private corporations instead of the government. This method has ensured that private corporations cannot run away from the responsibility of waste management, obligating all stakeholders, like importers and sellers, to internalize waste management techniques to reduce product costs and prevent punitive action.

Importance of Environmental Product Declarations

The internet has made a whirlwind of information accessible to everyone. People have expressed the need for quantified data regarding the effects of the products they purchase on the environment. This will help consumers make environmentally conscious decisions in their purchases, ensuring that a product's life cycle is always in mind. For this to happen, producers must provide quick access to all information about their product's life cycle. For this purpose, the Environmental Product Declaration was devised. The EPD ensures that the producers provide relevant, verified, and comparable information about the ecological impact of their product or service.

EPDs are derived from the ISO principles for Type III ecological declarations, thus holding international relevance. These EPDs also help in knowing important details about the product, like the process of raw material acquisition, energy consumption, the efficiency of the product, contents, chemical substances, emissions to air, soil, water, and generated waste.

Internal Carbon Pricing

The practice of internal carbon pricing is quickly gaining momentum in businesses. This method assigns a price to carbon emissions that can be attributed to the company. At the moment, more than 1200 companies worldwide have begun measuring and costing their carbon emissions to control the negative impact their product can have on the environment.

For companies that have initiated this policy, a monetary value is assigned to each business activity. This cost is then considered during investment decisions, incentivizing the corporation to consider programs and practices that do not result in high emissions levels. This also encourages designers and manufacturers to incorporate low-carbon materials and ensure that the product or service's impact on the environment is as little as possible.

Energy Efficiency

One of the best ways to ensure that a product wastes no energy or resources is to increase its energy efficiency. The efficiency of a product refers to its ability to perform at the minimum possible effort (energy). Often, malpractices encourage reductions in the product's energy efficiency so that it becomes less functional after a while, encouraging consumers to purchase the product once again to meet their needs. However, corporate climate change initiatives are trying to reverse the adverse effects of such greed. These green strategies have integrated the EP 100 initiative pledge to double their energy productivity (which refers to the dollars produced per unit of energy). This initiative alone can save more than 2 trillion dollars globally by 2030.

Data shows that big companies have made financial gains because of their renewed attention to energy efficiency. This has also had the added advantage of preventing greenhouse gas emissions. These strategies require the collaborative efforts of various internal operations of the company, their supply chains, and the nature of the product or service being offered. An assessment of the carbon footprint of a company can enable energy efficiency. Energy efficiency will also reduce a company's carbon footprint, as most of the energy wasted on products results in dangerous emissions. An environmentally inclusive company's leadership must be "SMART" (specific, measurable, accountable, realistic, and time-bound) in its energy-saving strategies. Mere tokenistic declarations are not enough, and the corporation should be able to show the results of using energy-efficient resources.

Innovative Finance

Producers of energy and, subsequently, energy-driven products offer their customers on-bill financing. This encourages consumers to consider making improvements in their energy consumption by incorporating equipment and products that are energy efficient to reduce the cost of their utility bills. It has become more common to see new landowners, or property owners consider the energy-efficient policies of their new place before acquiring it.

Big energy buyers also have to participate in green pricing programs, referred to as green tariffs. The countries like the United States of America have programs where consumers can buy energy at a premium if it comes from a renewable source. They can also issue a renewable energy certificate for renewable projects to avail of benefits. This innovative financial technique has encouraged several companies to switch to renewable energy sources like solar, wind, hydro, biomass power, geothermal energy, and landfill gas. Sustainability bonds (also known as green bonds) have become popular with corporations and money-lending institutions like banks. Environmentally conscious projects can avail of these sustainability bonds, which can function as capital and investment for institutions looking to invest in projects that acknowledge and reduce climate change. These bonds are commonly available for projects that involve the innovative creation of low-carbon products. Banks, corporations, or governments often issue these bonds. Sustainability bonds come with debt insurance, another incentive for ecologically sound companies with limited credit lines looking for capital for their renewable energy projects.

McDonald's is a fast-food chain that needs no introduction. The chain has more than 37,000 outlets worldwide, serving food to up to 70 million people daily! We ought to believe the financial and environmental decisions this company takes are pivotal worldwide. According to the report by Conservation International, the world's largest restaurant chain announced that it would reduce greenhouse emissions by 150 million metric tonnes by 2030. Steve Easterbrook, the CEO extraordinaire, announced that the company had undertaken a scenic-based target initiative to make this possible. In this move, they have launched a project to rebuild the destruction caused by one of their most widely consumed ingredients - beef. They will eliminate deforestation caused for the beef supply by restoring degraded lands - reducing the pressure on forest cover.

Moreover, the company aims to make all its packaging recyclable by 2025. Through these initiatives alone, McDonald's will be able to eliminate the number of emissions that a country like Belgium produces! The company also has a no-deforestation policy allowing at least 30% of all mitigation action required to prevent climate change.

Steps for Corporates to Reduce Their Environmental Footprint

1. Reduce Your Emissions

Your emissions may constitute a minor portion of the total emissions, but they are usually easier to cut because they are directly under the company's control.

- Improve the Energy efficiency of buildings.
- Implement passive cooling/heating technologies wherever possible.
- Reduce energy, material, and resource waste in all operations.
- Reduce emissions and expenses by optimizing the use of building space in all operations.
- Meet the energy demand with your renewable energy systems.
- Purchase renewable energy through power purchase agreements.

2. Reduce Your Value Chain Emissions

Emissions from upstream and downstream activities related to the reporting company's operations are called value chain emissions. They typically account for most of a company's total footprint and must thus be acknowledged. For example, IKEA's value chain emissions account for 97% of the company's overall emissions.

- Map out the carbon emissions linked with your value chain to determine the most significant ones and begin rigorously tracking them.
- Evaluate and choose materials, transport, and product suppliers based on emission data and climate strategy transparency, and collaborate with other industry partners to strengthen purchase requirements.
- Create a plan to reduce commuting trip emissions, such as encouraging and financing low-carbon travel to and from work and allowing employees to work from local green office hubs closer to home.
- Incorporate strong climate criteria into your research and development, product, and service design processes to increase the energy performance of sold products, use less material, recycle and employ low-carbon materials, and construct low-carbon and circular economy solutions for customers.

3. Integrate Climate into Your Business Strategy

Consider renewable energy and energy storage, plant-based sustainable food production, energy-positive buildings, vehicle, space, and object sharing, zero-carbon materials, and material circularity. Business models will need to shift from ownership to users, from product-based to service-based, and from linear to circular - all of which will be possible by digital technology. Your business concept primarily determines your contribution. Through vehicle sharing, circular economies, and close-to-home tourism, you may assist in altering consumer trends in a more sustainable direction.

Suppose your services and products influence consumer and business decisions, such as social and e-commerce platforms, advertising, and management consulting; in that case, you can enable and encourage customers to make climate-friendly decisions. You will want to be at the forefront of this transformation to maintain your competitive advantage. This may necessitate a change in your business model. Plan your company's net-zero future. Define what that looks like and what needs to be accomplished for your firm to get there.

Discover new company prospects by investigating new offerings and business methods and engaging environmentally sensitive customer groups.

Determine which corporate activities must be phased out to prevent negative climate consequences. In addition to halving global emissions by 2030, natural carbon sinks such as forests and wetlands must be safeguarded and restored to maintain the climate. The corporate sectors now causing emissions must take responsibility for accelerating the necessary investments. As a result, emissions that cannot be rapidly eliminated should preferably be offset by investment in high-quality programs that remove carbon from the atmosphere.

Investing in carbon credit projects is a solution that you should use to complement deep decarbonization. It should not be a substitute for reducing emissions and creating new solutions to reduce global heating. It is important to carefully decide where carbon credit should be purchased to ensure impact. These projects should be aligned with sustainable development goals and should meet high standards. Some such projects are as follows:

- Collaborate strategically with key partners to build circular and carbon-free value chains.
- If your services and products influence consumer and business decisions, such as digital platforms, advertising, and management consulting, ensure that your services enable and

encourage your customers to make climate-friendly purchases and investment decisions.

- Consider making qualitative and quantitative assessments of your solutions' climate impact and setting measurable goals.
- Consider accounting for a price on carbon to make climate an integral part of your investment procedures.
- Determine the remaining emissions from your company and value chain which cannot be immediately removed.
- Purchase carbon credits that are at least equal to these emissions and use the proceeds to fund high-quality, third-party certified projects that remove carbon from the atmosphere or programs that avoid emissions. To assure climate effect, it is best to over-invest, potentially doubling your calculations, to account for uncertainties.
- Disclose carbon credit projects separately in your annual reporting.
- Check in on those projects to ensure that they are delivering on their promises.
- If you apply carbon-neutral or climate-positive concepts, follow solid recommendations and standards.

4. Influence Climate Action In Society

To become a societal climate leader, you must leverage your company's network and wider sphere of influence to support and accelerate climate action. This can be accomplished by influencing and collaborating with consumers and suppliers, employees, industry, government, cities, research organizations, and non-governmental organizations (NGOs) in areas other than your corporate interests. It could include proposing or requiring regulatory changes to enable quick economic and behavioral change, raising customer understanding about climate change, developing solutions, and sharing best practices with your business and community. Some steps could be as follows:

- Develop and invest in sectoral industry roadmaps and define and drive the required strategies and actions for halving emissions and reaching net zero in collaboration with customers, suppliers, and other partners.
- In partnership with customers, suppliers, and other partners, develop and invest in sectoral industry roadmaps and identify and drive the necessary strategies and activities for halving emissions and reaching net zero.
- Persuade local and national policymakers to increase climate action. Advocate for regulatory bodies to promote industry-wide action.
- Educate your board and management regularly on climate, the SDGs, and your company's positive and negative contributions.
- Help your employees and owners start halving their emissions.

Final Thoughts

The role of industries in climate change has come under global scrutiny, leading to a heightened focus on the life cycle assessment of products. Consumers are increasingly considering the environmental impact of products from their production to disposal. In this chapter, we explored several ways in which corporations can contribute to building a sustainable future.

Assessing the life cycle of a product allows producers to identify areas of environmental degradation and prioritize improvements. By understanding the hot spots in their supply chains and production processes, companies can implement strategies to minimize resource exploitation and reduce their carbon footprint.

Finding alternatives to production practices that rely heavily on natural resources is crucial. Exploring sustainable materials, renewable energy sources and adopting more efficient manufacturing techniques can significantly reduce environmental impact.

Financial practices that incentivize climate-friendly practices can play a pivotal role in driving change. Offering incentives, grants, or subsidies to companies that adopt sustainable practices encourages green thinking and fosters innovation in the market. This financial support can facilitate the development and adoption of environmentally friendly technologies and practices.

In today's market, it is easier than ever to differentiate a product based on its environmental performance. Consumers are increasingly seeking out products that prioritize sustainability and contribute positively to the environment. By aligning their products with eco-friendly values, companies can stand out from the competition and attract a growing customer base that values sustainability.

In conclusion, industries have a critical role to play in addressing climate change. Assessing product life cycles, seeking alternatives to resource-intensive practices, and implementing financial incentives for sustainability are important steps companies can take. By prioritizing environmental stewardship, businesses can make a significant contribution to building a sustainable future and differentiate themselves in the market.

4
LOCAL GOVERNMENTS

"Climate change is not just an environmental issue; it is a matter of social justice, human rights, and economic stability. We must address it holistically for a better world."

Dealing with conversations around climate change and its impact is no longer a choice. It is imperative to find solutions for our survival, especially as members of the Third World. Environmental predictions indicate that countries that belong to the third world, including India, Bangladesh, Indonesia, etc., shall be the first to suffer the consequences of unprecedented climate change.

The call for action against accelerated climate change would involve having conversations about livelihoods and social communities. We must observe how we live our lives and whether we can find sustainable alternatives for leading our lives. These alternatives need to be accessible and quick so we can implement them across all sections of society as soon as possible. This will involve the cooperation of local, central, and national governments and an environmentally-motivated perspective among citizens.

Vulnerability Assessment for Climate Change

Vulnerability refers to how susceptible a region or a community is to the negative impacts of accelerated climate change. This varies across societies, labor sectors, and areas of a country. To bring about change, we need to assess how different parts of the world will be affected by the specific changes happening in their environment. A country's vulnerability comparison will vary across local indicators, like the groups of less developed regions and less developed communities. We will also need to compare the rate at which "progress" occurs in the human development of two areas that might previously have had similar economic statuses. At the state level, assessment of vulnerability would involve the creation of development policies and, further, specifying policy actions that could reduce climate change.

Sectoral assessments of climate change can provide us with the details required to create necessary and strategic development plans. At the local level, vulnerable communities can be identified, and policies can be implemented to help them. The poor people of our country are the most susceptible, and climate change is bound to increase poverty. That is why the adverse effects of climate change will affect developing nations and the poor of developing countries the most. Developing nations are bound by their tropical weather conditions, geographical location, and high dependence on natural resources. The poor people of these developing nations are vulnerable as they have the least resources to combat the ill effects of climate change. Their capacity to adapt is also a lot less due to reduced awareness.

Effects of Climate Change in the Developing World

As of now, data scientists and researchers have speculated that extreme climate events' occurrence, frequency, intensity, and duration will be dominant in the developing world. These climate extremes include heat waves. Floods, droughts, heavy precipitation, and other change will also gradually affect the livelihoods of the people living in these regions. These researchers have also predicted that India will bear significant climate change consequences. At the moment as well, several parts of the country are experiencing severe heat waves, affecting the already vulnerable sections of society. Increasing use of land, the concretization of land, and changing weather conditions are some of the many factors that have caused these exhausting heat waves across the Indian subcontinent.

According to research, the higher emissions in India will put a population of about 160 to 200 million people in danger by exposing them to heatwaves for extended periods. This will affect people as we advance into the next decade. Even worse, more than half of the people affected by these heatwaves shall not have access to relief measures like air conditioning and permanent shelter.

Moreover, outdoor work is responsible for more than half of India's gross domestic product. The increase in heat would limit outdoor production, leading to the exploitation of workers and an economic deficit. The current heat waves in the spring will substantially impact the country's wheat harvest, a source of significant concern for farmers and intermediaries involved in the agricultural world. Labour productivity will reduce drastically in the upcoming years in India.

Research has indicated that India could effectively lose more than 30% of its current daylight working hours, disproportionately impacting the lives of those who work outdoors and the poor people who do not have access to cooling systems. Even for the world's wealthiest countries, there is an expected decline in productivity due to increasing climate change. For developed countries, there could be a 1-5% decline in working hours whereas, for the developing countries of the world, there could be a decline of about 5-10% in the total working hours. These estimations are for the year 2050. However, if the rate of emissions remains the same or if it increases (due to the prevalence of ignorant leadership worldwide), we will see climate change impact people's lives even sooner.

Adaptive Capacity

The Government of India released the National Action Plan for

Climate Change (NAPCC) in 2008. This project aimed to mitigate and adapt to combat the adverse impacts of climate change.

According to this official action plan, the government of India is supposed to undertake eight missions to mitigate climate change. According to this plan, India will work with other developing nations to reduce carbon emissions effectively. Local climate action, sustainable energy alternatives, and urban planning are closely interconnected. The most optimum way in which we can introduce real change in terms of climate change is through awareness among the masses and by developing and implementing new policies.

Climate change mitigation is not a one-size-fits-all method. The combination of institutional, legal, and political tools accessible to public decision-makers varies by location, as do the effects of climate change. Local, regional, and state government decision-makers must participate actively in climate change preparation since climate change effects are felt and understood most clearly in their jurisdictions.

Focus on Energy Efficiency

The first step in achieving sustainability in Energy is Energy Savings. The next important aspect is Energy Efficiency, followed by replacing the conventional energy source with renewable energy. The easiest ways to achieve sustainability goals are to save energy and improve energy efficiency. These methods can be employed for ongoing production processes and production processes that are in the planning stage and can be morphed into more environmentally conscious projects. Local governments must work with their communities' political and economic contexts while assessing energy needs and executing sustainable projects. From this perspective, moving to renewable energy is essential, backed by other benefits such as local job creation, stable energy pricing, and ensuring sufficient power for the community. A unique way local government around the world have approached the topic of energy conservation is through their engagement with the corporate world. However, despite the popularity of such an approach, environmental consciousness remains a volunteer effort. There are very few rewards and policies in place that are punitive towards energy wastage or encourage sustainable practices.

At the moment, the degree of influence these environmentally conscious practices have on the country's people is very subjective. Data has revealed that the impact of these practices vary from country to country, region to region. Despite the differences in implementation and influence, it is observed that the practices of a local council, as well as the decisions made by them for the wellbeing of a community, have the most immediate impact on the lives of the people.

Local governments typically have a wide range of abilities and influence that can be leveraged to guide community change. Council decisions and regulations, for example, can be adopted to help drive and regulate change within the municipality. These can also be important to the entire community or target groups such as people, businesses, and industry. There is a significant opportunity to lead, advise, and stimulate action to minimize the primary causes of pollution in the community's energy, building, transportation, water, and waste sectors.

Local governments can impact the energy efficiency of new and existing buildings in their communities. They can put policies in place ranging from setting goals and leading by example, implementing rules and performance systems, providing financial and non-financial reinforcements, and assisting stakeholders and improving the business case for pursuing or financing energy or water efficiency. Many local governments generate energy. Many of the day-to-day activities that determine the amount of energy used and waste generated by their community can be controlled or influenced by local governments, ranging from land use and zoning decisions to control over building codes and licenses, infrastructure investments, municipal service delivery, and management of schools, parks, and recreation areas. They have data access and can examine the energy consumption trends of various regions and sub-regions to determine the cause of excessive consumption. It's worth looking into how local Governments can impact citizen behavior that directly affects climate change, such as transportation options, energy consumption habits, and general consumer preferences—determining where greenhouse gases are released and alternatives for changing tactics or systems to reduce emissions is a crucial step.

Awareness

Voluntary action has had a significant impact on the climate change movement. Access to the internet has introduced the people of the world to how our actions are depleting the Earth's resources. The internet has taught us to understand the role of affirmative steps and preventive measures in controlling the impact of climate change on our lives. However, despite access to the internet, climate change remains unknown to a vast majority of people in countries like India. The kind of awareness local governments can bring through their access to communication channels is impeccable.

The local government must identify the community's main stakeholders from all areas of life. Local governments can be in an ideal position to inform, mobilize, and involve the local populace and various stakeholders in various activities. This involvement is required for local climate action to be successful. There will be no change unless people are engaged. The goal should be to involve as many residents as possible, the entire business sector and local industries, and all political parties, municipal personnel, and local stakeholder groups. Community awareness and involvement are essential components of local climate action success, which may be achieved by addressing a broad target audience on various themes ranging from waste to energy use at home and the workplace to personal mobility choices.

Resilient Infrastructure

The damage caused by climate change to our infrastructure can significantly impact developing and underdeveloped nations' employment and economic conditions. Imagine building industries and infrastructure for these industries from scratch in a region already impoverished due to gross economic inequalities.

The world observed the severe effect of drought-induced power outages in countries like Zimbabwe and Zambia, which significantly degrades the quality of life (water, health, supply chains, and businesses were affected drastically). Surveys have revealed that Tanzania alone lost $101 million (a whopping 0.3% of their annual GDP) because of the power shortage caused by excessive rain and floods, in addition to a $150 million loss due to lack of transport during flooding.

The most heart-wrenching result of such disasters is that Governments must divert public funds to rebuild instead of investing in new infrastructure to compensate for existing deficits. This leads to what researchers have termed the "infrastructure trap, " leading to vicious cycles of extreme climate events. These events have disrupted the lives of people and halted economic growth.

There is an immediate need to invest in and build climate-resilient infrastructure. Climate resilient infrastructure is planned, designed, built, and operated in a way that anticipates, prepares for, and adapts to changing climate conditions. It can also withstand, respond to, and recover rapidly from disruptions caused by these climate conditions.

One of the simplest ways to resist the negative impact of climate change on our infrastructure is by ensuring that they are located in areas that are less vulnerable to climate hazards. For example, we must thoroughly inspect the climate impact of new businesses and their respective infrastructure. Avoiding the setup of heavy infrastructure on flood plains is one of the many ways we can avoid destruction. One of the many ways early interventions can help prevent the loss of road infrastructure is by changing the composition of elements used in constructing roads to ensure that they do not deform in high temperatures. Building seawalls and permeable paving surfaces can help reduce water accumulation due to heavy rainfall.

Green Infrastructure

The frequency and intensity of rainfall have increased in the past decade. The increasing demand for land to build more residential and commercial zones to meet the demand of the growing population in the urban area has led to extensive building activity near lakes, streams, and wetlands. The flood buffer offered by these natural spaces has been lost.

Cities are expanding, but water bodies are shrinking. The waterbodies also have to grow in proportion to the increase in built-up areas to match with and to be able to manage the rainwater. Climate change-driven rainfall variability is increasing, with rainfall equivalent to monthly/seasonal averages falling within a few days. There is a need for Urban planning departments of Central and State Governments to focus on effective flood mitigation in their development plan and build disaster-resilient infrastructure.

Historically, communities have employed grey infrastructure—systems of gutters, pipes, and tunnels—to transport stormwater away from our homes and into treatment plants or directly into local bodies of water. The grey infrastructure of many places is outdated, and its capacity to manage significant volumes of stormwater is dwindling across the country. The existing urban development with grey infrastructure needs to be integrated with the new blue-green approach by using natural systems to bolster their capacity to manage stormwater and thereby become more resilient.

Parks and green covers reduce or slow down the stormwater runoff while the water bodies hold the rainwater. The hybrid approaches of porous pavements, bioswales, rain gardens, and water retention planters along the streets can be a part of water-prudent landscapes. Instead of flooding the low-lying areas in heavy rainfall, the city parks and playgrounds can act as makeshift ponds to hold the runoff. Ecosystem-based approaches using natural infrastructure to design adaptation measures are important alternatives to be considered alongside structural adaptation measures.

Green infrastructural strategies are slowly becoming more

popular than they were before. These strategies involve a planned network of natural and semi-natural areas alongside other environmental resources designed and managed by ecosystem services.

Use of Biofuels

Exploitation and burning of fossil fuels is the primary cause of pollution. The use of fossil fuels in creating industrial emissions, burning human waste, vehicle exhausts, construction activities, and so much more can be limited and even eliminated from our lives. A survey conducted by Harvard in the United States has confirmed that 30% of all mortalities in India have been due to a direct impact of air pollution, a result of the overconsumption of fossil fuels. You can read about these findings in the 'Environmental Research' of February 2021.

In addition, at the moment, more than 20% of all fatalities worldwide are directly related to rising pollution. Despite these ominous warning signs, fossil fuels continue to be our primary source of energy across all sectors of survival. Currently, fossil fuels are providing 80% of the total energy required to keep the world running the way it is. Moreover, along with energy production, fossil fuels are also used to produce several other items we use daily- plastic and steel products being one of the most common examples. The uncontrolled burning and consumption of fossil fuels have resulted in 89% of the world's total carbon emissions, causing global warming. These fossil fuels include oil and coal, two of today's most used energy creation and consumption resources. Environment experts have concluded that we need to reduce coal consumption by more than 50% if we wish to control the rise of global temperatures. If we do not limit the global rise in temperature to 1.5 °C, we will suffer dire environmental consequences.

In June 2018, the Government of India released a new biofuel policy. Through this intervention, the government has indicated a goal to blend 20% ethanol in petrol, and 5% of biodiesel will be mixed with regular diesel by 2030. The environmental authorities of India have taken several steps to introduce 2nd generation biofuels in India, as previously, only 2% ethanol was blended, and only 0.1% biodiesel was blended with diesel. Using biofuels can help us become energy sufficient as a country and energy-efficient with climate change in mind. Fuels developed from biomass can be used to construct roads, maintain water and air transport, etc. More importantly, the shift to biofuel will help boost the rural economy by providing more alternative jobs for people, helping us develop our economy.

India is an agricultural country. Innovations in technology and supply chain systems of agriculture are a need of the hour. We can use them to make ethanol from food crops, a technique popular in countries such as Brazil and the USA for more than four decades now. India has been producing ethanol through home-grown technology using sugar crops.

This raises the debate about food versus fuel in the technological world. Policymakers often pick a side between food and biofuel production when addressing the population's needs. However, innovations in technology have helped us out of this dilemma. At the moment, we have created 2nd generation technologies that can help us produce biofuels like ethanol from wasted grains and other leftovers from farms. Creating biofuels from destroyed food crops can help us in food preservation and fuel preservation, a landmark step in the world of sustainable development. It is imperative to consider biofuels as not just an alternative to current fuels but also the foundation of a new beginning in sustainable technology. Using agriculturally sourced biofuels indicates that we can create new forms of sustainable energy through technological innovation.

Not only will this help in managing waste, but this technique of producing biofuels from waste will also help generate passive income for farmers who are reeling under the current economic crisis. Thus, biofuels will become the center of a new, sufficient and efficient rural economy, helping generate energy for various industrial and agricultural processes. Farmers will not need to depend on the local administration to get power to run their machines. Nor would they have to spend any part of their income to obtain fuel to run those machines - they can become independent in their profession and generate surplus income.

Waste to Energy Plants

Ever wondered what happens to the trash from our dustbins once it leaves our homes? Waste management is one of the most significant issues plaguing India's cities and towns. The lack of appropriate infrastructure to manage waste has led to large landfills full of garbage that is left unattended. You will often find young human scavengers struggling to find a valuable item or two from the heaps of waste discarded near their shelter. The waste-to-energy plant is a technological innovation that helps produce energy from waste. However, the use of this technology is not so simple. One is expected to know the composition of the waste through incentivization. Waste released from households has to be tested, and the composition of the solid waste has to be specified for the technology to be applied appropriately.

Ongoing surveys have revealed that around 50-55% of the waste generated is organic, 11% is made of paper, 13-14% is made of plastic in the form of packaging, and less than 6% is made of permanent substances like glass and metal. The remaining is made of inert materials. The first step to producing energy from such waste is to segregate it. Once you have all the organic waste in one place, you can generate biogas, and among the others, you can recycle products made from plastic, steel, and glass.

However, the most crucial step for this system to work smoothly is segregation at the source, an action that is often neglected by our households and waste collection channels.

Thus, urban local bodies need to invest in preparing an action plan for waste-to-energy production for their small cities and towns. The model mentioned above can be implemented successfully with smaller populations. Hence, we must rely on the multiple levels of leadership that govern our city to coordinate and enable this essential waste management process. These urban local bodies should work according to solid waste management rules created in 2016. An important thing to note about waste-to-energy conversion is that the functioning of these plants is often avoided because of the expense. Landfills and waste to energy plants can be costly. Hence, we not only need to introduce waste to energy plants, but we also need to reduce waste production. We must ensure that we do not overconsume our resources because even sustainable practices can come with drawbacks like the emission of dangerous gases.

Carbon Sequestration and Carbon Offsets

Members and consumers of industrial production are wondering what could be the affirmative solution to climate change. Preventive measures such as waste reduction and management are already in place; however, how can we incentivize large-scale affirmative action regarding climate change? Organizations are beginning to practice carbon offsetting schemes and carbon sequestration to answer this question. These practices are helping undo the damage caused by consuming resources that can destroy our planet's environment.

What is Carbon Sequestration?

Carbon sequestration is capturing, securing, and storing carbon dioxide from the atmosphere. This process works on the principle of stabilizing carbon in solid or dissolved forms to prevent its emissions into the atmosphere. Large amounts of carbon in the air (in the form of oxides and monoxides) are one of the many causes of rising global temperatures.

This process has been celebrated and encouraged worldwide for its ability to reduce an organization's carbon footprint. Carbon sequestration can be done biologically and geologically as well.

Biological Carbon Sequestration

This form of carbon sequestration refers to storing carbon in biological entities like grasslands, forests, oceans, and the soil. Oceans are large reservoirs of greenhouse emissions. Currently, 25% of humanity's carbon dioxide has been absorbed by our oceans. The process of balancing the composition of oceans is complex. The oceans absorb and release carbon dioxide into the air, forming positive atmospheric flux.

A negative atmospheric flux is the phenomenon of excess absorption of carbon dioxide by the oceans. Nutrient-rich plants from cold regions of the world can absorb more carbon dioxide and are hence referred to as carbon sinks. It is predicted that before the end of the century, our oceans will comprise carbon dioxide, changing the chemistry of the water entirely - making it very acidic. Photosynthesis enables the conversion of atmospheric carbon dioxide into soil organic carbon. Effective land management can help expand the soil's ability to absorb carbon dioxide from the atmosphere. In addition to organic carbon, the ground can also store carbon in the form of other compounds like carbonates. Carbonates can function as excellent reservoirs of carbon because they can absorb at faster rates and higher volumes. In addition to the soil, our ecosystem also maintains a natural system of checks and balances through forests. Approximately 25% of global carbon dioxide is absorbed by our forests, grasslands, and other natural areas. Increased deforestation for human activities has led to the dissolution of these carbon sinks, increasing global atmospheric carbon dioxide.

Grasslands are highly effective as they are less affected by natural calamities like droughts and floods. Moreover, they emit a lot less carbon dioxide than they absorb.

The majority of the carbon in grasslands is sequestered underground. When they burn, the carbon in the roots and soil remains fixed. Although forests can store more carbon, grasslands are more robust in uncertain conditions caused by climate change.

Geological Carbon Sequestration

This is another essential process of eliminating carbon from our atmosphere. Here, the sequestration process is completed with the help of geological formations like rocks. In most geological sequestration processes, carbon dioxide is trapped from industrial sources (like manufacturing industries) and injected into natural porous rocks. This method is effective as it can help reduce carbon emissions in the atmosphere and also help us replenish fossil fuels already on our planet.

Technological Carbon Sequestration

At the moment, scientists worldwide are finding new ways to eliminate and store carbon dioxide from our atmosphere. The production of graphene is one among several such sustainable practices. In this way, we can reuse the already available carbon to produce more graphene, an essential raw material for the production of smartphones and other gadgets. Though Energy-intensive processes like direct air capture are becoming increasingly popular, they are still too costly to implement on a mass scale. Carbon sequestration is a necessary part of several industries now. It can help maintain nature's balance. We cannot afford to neglect our emissions anymore, as the impact is already visible on our natural ecosystems. For example, the increase in carbon dioxide absorbed by our oceans has led to a rise in the acidity of oceanic water (which has, in turn, affected marine life adversely).

Carbon Farming

India is the world's second-largest producer of staple foods such as rice, wheat, groundnuts, fruits, and vegetables. Agriculture is an important sector in India, accounting for about 20% of total GDP, employing more than half of the country's 1.4 billion people, and providing a primary source of income for more than 70% of rural households. However, it is a significant contributor to greenhouse gas emissions due to deforestation, land usage, and rice agriculture.

During COP26, India announced its five-point climate change

policy, which includes reducing one billion tons of carbon by 2030, reducing the carbon intensity of GDP by 45% by 2030, and achieving net-zero emissions by 2070. While agriculture is regarded as a primary contributor to greenhouse gas emissions, it can also be a part of the solution.

Farmlands have the potential to store up to 1.2 billion tonnes of carbon and could offset 4% of average yearly GHG emissions for the rest of the century if the correct techniques are used. Carbon farming is a method of agricultural management that promotes the land to collect and store more greenhouse gases rather than releasing them into the atmosphere.

Carbon credits, recognized emission reductions from climate-positive projects, are swiftly becoming popular to encourage sustainable company practices and assist in achieving global net-zero targets. While most carbon credit initiatives are dedicated to renewable energy and reforestation, there is a growing interest in the concept of 'carbon farming.' These programs aim to strengthen agriculture's involvement in climate protection by encouraging offset generation through soil carbon sequestration to exchange these carbon offsets.

Microsoft, for example, recently agreed to purchase $2 million in carbon credits from an American farming cooperative. At the same time, US Vice President Biden has proposed a "carbon bank" to compensate farmers for adopting regenerative agriculture practices.

Agriculture-related carbon credit schemes have been mainly limited to large-scale holdings in developed economies, where farmers have greater access to information, technology, and the requisite automation and equipment. However, the potential for an effect in the developing world — home to hundreds of millions of small-acreage farmers — is enormous. There must be a simpler validation and verification process for carbon credits to scale projects faster and support sustainable practices.

Carbon Farming Project Launched In India

A new project will assist farmers in increasing their revenue while also storing carbon in their soil. The carbon farming project will begin with 20 farmers in two districts of Maharashtra in India, compensating farmers for increased soil organic carbon. These farmers cultivate rice and other cover crops using no-till techniques. Shekar Bhadsavale, a California-educated progressive farmer from Neral, and Emmanuel D'Silva, an agriculture and environment expert from Mumbai who previously worked at the World Bank, founded the project. A 1% increase in soil organic carbon in one acre is equivalent to storing 18 metric tons of CO_2 beneath our feet. "Agriculture, if done correctly, can give a stronger answer to the climate challenge than other industries," said D'Silva.

Individuals, commercial corporations, and non-governmental organizations (NGOs) concerned about climate change would reward farmers for increased soil carbon under the program. Carbon Farming is more than just using soil management practices on a farm to sequester carbon. It is also about farmers and planters working together to enhance the local environment!

Carbon Offsetting

Like carbon sequestration, the guiding principle for carbon offsetting is the desire to balance our carbon footprint.

This process involves the creation of environmental projects around the world that can help in this mission. This process is encouraged by using an emissions trading scheme where clean energy technologies are used to reduce carbon credit. As an organization, you can offset your entire facility or a particular industry activity to neutralize your impact on the environment. This involves the simple process of visiting the offset website, where you can assess the environmental impact of all forms of business activities (like taking flights, etc.). Once you have set your activity's effect, you can pay the offset company, which will use the funds to reduce emissions in another part of the world.

Usually, offset schemes are determined through XYZ rupees per tonne of carbon dioxide released into the atmosphere. You can undertake this initiative to undo the damage caused during a family vacation or a business trip and make sure that somewhere, in some part of the world, you can undo the damage done to our climate. Earlier, carbon offsetting schemes were criticized by many environmentalists. People claim that the mere act of planting trees could not be an effective way in which we can undo the environmental damage done by our activities. George Monbiot famously compared this process with the ancient Catholic practice of "selling sins" to prevent them.

Since many offsetting companies have switched to more effective methods like creating clean energy projects around the world, this involves the distribution of energy-efficient kitchen stoves to procure methane gas from landfills. However, this process continues to be critiqued for the lack of accessibility for people from all classes. It has been called a mere indulgence for wealthy people who do not want to feel guilty about their environmentally exploitative practices.

Empower the Consumer

In order to drive the manufacturing industry towards reducing its environmental footprint, it is important for governments and authorities to mandate the disclosure of a product's environmental impact. This can be achieved by requiring manufacturers to publish the environmental footprint of their products on the packaging or through other accessible means. By providing consumers with this information, they can make more informed choices based on the environmental impact of the products they purchase.

Currently, consumers face challenges in identifying products that have a lower environmental impact due to the lack of available data. By including the environmental footprint alongside the ingredients on product packaging, consumers will be empowered to make conscious choices that align with their sustainability values.

Revealing the environmental footprint of products serves multiple purposes. Firstly, it allows consumers to select products that align with their environmental concerns, fostering demand for more sustainable options. Secondly, it incentivizes manufacturers to improve their production processes, reduce resource consumption, and minimize environmental harm in order to meet consumer preferences and remain competitive in the market.

Transparent and accessible information about a product's environmental impact not only empowers consumers but also encourages a shift towards more sustainable practices within the manufacturing industry as a whole. It supports the collective effort to create a market where sustainability is a driving force, leading to reduced resource consumption, lower emissions, and a more environmentally conscious society.

By providing consumers with the necessary information to make informed choices, we can promote a marketplace that values sustainability and encourages manufacturers to prioritize environmental stewardship in their operations.

Final Thoughts

Throughout history, collaboration has proven to be vital in driving global movements for positive change. Progressive movements that have uplifted societies and brought about significant transformations have been fueled by the solidarity of individuals across various social, economic, and cultural backgrounds. In the face of climate change, this collaborative spirit is more crucial than ever.

Local governments and authorities play a significant role in addressing climate change and fostering sustainable practices within their communities. They have the power to implement policies, regulations, and initiatives that promote climate-friendly practices and create a supportive environment for change. By working together, individuals, communities, and local institutions can discover innovative and effective ways to mitigate the damage caused by our harmful activities.

Raising awareness about climate change is a key component of collective action. Spreading awareness from door to door, engaging in community discussions, and organizing educational programs can help ensure that everyone understands the urgency and importance of addressing climate change. This shared understanding can foster a sense of responsibility and motivate individuals to adopt sustainable behaviors in their daily lives.

Introducing climate-friendly practices in local institutions is another impactful step. Implementing measures such as adopting biofuels, promoting carbon sequestration, and offsetting carbon emissions can contribute to reducing the environmental impact of these institutions. By taking affirmative action at the local level, we can inspire broader change and encourage others to follow suit.

While affirmative actions are crucial, preventive measures should not be overlooked. It is essential to consider the long-term implications of our actions and prioritize strategies that prevent further harm to the environment. This includes measures like reducing greenhouse gas emissions, protecting natural resources, conserving biodiversity, and adopting sustainable land-use practices.

In conclusion, collaboration is the key to effectively addressing climate change. By joining forces, sharing knowledge, and taking affirmative and preventive actions at the local level, we can work towards undoing the damage caused by our harmful activities. Through collective effort and a shared commitment to sustainability, we can create a resilient and environmentally conscious world for present and future generations.

5
SUSTAINABLE COMMUNITIES

"The best way to predict future is to create it."
- Peter Drucker

The global urbanization trend is progressing rapidly, with projections indicating that over 70% of the world's population will reside in cities by 2050. However, the current state of cities is marked by densely populated living spaces and a relentless demand for vital resources. It is crucial to contemplate the potential consequences of our resource consumption patterns on the future urban landscape.

Visualizing the future of cities with continued resource consumption at the current rate raises important questions. Will we have enough space to accommodate the growing population? Will there be sufficient resources to meet the escalating demands for food, water, and energy? How will the environment and ecosystems be affected by this unrestrained resource exploitation?

Environmentalists have warned the world about the results of such catastrophic consumption in the cities. They have recommended a move towards building more sustainable communities to combat this problem. Developers should consider creating projects where people can coexist with tiny urban forests in the form of 'sponge cities.' These cities would ideally be able to soak up floodwater and shall be composed of vertical forests that seem to touch the sky. There can be no future for our cities if they do not become sustainable.

What are Sustainable Communities?

Creating a safe and well-functioning sustainable future for cities has reached the top of every country's green agenda. Cities continue to remain the economic center for regions in a country, providing stable livelihoods and a chance to overcome social limitations for one and all. Sustainable cities shall be able to do the same, however, this time with the well-being of our planet in mind as well. Sustainable cities built with materials, spaces, and ecosystems effectively can help reduce the negative impact of infrastructure and buildings on the environment. These cities shall primarily be able to do so because of their ability to optimize the efficiency of the goods and services that they consume.

We cannot imagine a sustainable future without accepting the interconnectedness of our society, economy, and environment we live in. It is the community's responsibility to address the fact that its members are consuming more than the resources available, causing major environmental distress. Moreover, a community must also be mindful of the rate at which resources can be replaced naturally. In the case of urban spaces, the quick expansion of human settlements can cause an exponential increase in the consumption of natural resources. Thus, once the immediate resources are emptied, we rely on materials that have to be fetched from far-off distances, which in turn causes the use of more resources for transportation and distribution. However, this can be avoided if we give an impetus to the co-existence of natural lands, efficient transportation for all, and overall energy savings. Hence, if we wish to make our futures more sustainable, we need to make sure of the following:

- Social equity and inclusiveness
- Economically productive cities

- Creating harmony between the natural and artificial environment
- Preserving the history of the cities
- Developing cities for all generations
- Sustainable Residential Communities/Societies

It is easier for people to follow a sustainable and conscious lifestyle when they live collectively in communities that are designed and built, integrating sustainability principles.

As part of my professional work, I have been conducting sustainability audits and providing recommendations to communities in order to reduce their carbon footprint. During my visits to various communities, I have consistently observed a common issue in gated communities: a lack of emphasis on energy efficiency in their design. Additionally, these communities often lack dedicated spaces for waste segregation, hindering residents' ability to recycle the waste they generate.

One significant challenge arises during the implementation phase. While in the design stage, there are typically two or three decision-makers responsible for determining the facilities and features of the project. However, once the project is handed over and occupied, a multitude of individuals with diverse perspectives are involved in decision-making, even for seemingly minor choices. This can complicate the implementation of various sustainability features that were not accounted for during the initial design phase.

Here are examples of two projects at different stages and infrastructure to explain the scenario:

Project 1: In a residential community consisting of 450 families, where I used to reside, there was a notable absence of a designated area for waste segregation. However, a group of environmentally conscious residents took the initiative to address this issue. They embarked on a mission to raise awareness among their neighbors about the importance of recycling and the consequences of sending mixed waste to municipal facilities. Additionally, they collaborated with recycling vendors who were able to collect waste from a central location.

Despite their efforts, only 30% of the residents agreed to segregate their waste into dry and wet categories. The community lacked a communal space, and the Management Committee was reluctant to bear the cost of employing an additional staff member. Given these circumstances, it becomes challenging to envision residential communities willingly investing in infrastructural changes such as solar panels and water conservation plants within the premises. Even after two years of the committee's establishment, the community of only 450 families has been unable to initiate a waste segregation campaign.

Project 2: On the other hand, there is an apartment building specifically designed to harness rainwater to fulfill 30% of its domestic water demand. The building is equipped with rainwater tanks and treatment systems that ensure the water can be reused. Furthermore, the building incorporates a Sewage Treatment Plant (STP) to treat water to a level suitable for flushing and landscaping purposes. Solar power is employed to meet the energy requirements of common areas. The building also features a dedicated space for organic waste composting and a waste segregation room. They have established partnerships with waste management vendors to handle all types of waste effectively.

This building exemplifies a comprehensive plan and strategy, starting from the collection of segregated waste from each household to its proper disposal. Even before residents move in, workshops are conducted to educate them on following the guidelines and the positive impact of adopting a sustainable lifestyle. In this case, residents are not given the option to mix their waste, as the building's bylaws clearly state that housekeeping will not collect mixed waste. The residents benefit greatly from the established infrastructure and support, making it easier for them to embrace sustainable practices compared to the community described in the first example.

The key factor we must acknowledge and bear in mind during our sustainability endeavours is that there is no one-size-fits-all solution to the issue of climate change. Many advocates of change overlook the fact that countries like India grapple with significant economic and social disparities. As we strive for sustainability, our solutions must be tailored to align with our existing structures to create a more inclusive and equitable future, different from our current unequal and challenging circumstances.

For instance, advocating for the conversion of all hot water sources to sustainable solar power in institutions and homes is a commendable effort. However, this approach may not be suitable for houses in areas where occupants visit primarily for leisure, such as secondary or weekend homes with low occupancy rates. In such cases, sustainable projects require a different infrastructure tailored to their unique needs. It is essential to look beyond the monetary cost of a project and consider its suitability and practicality in various contexts when exploring sustainable alternatives in our lives.

Furthermore, merely replacing infrastructure with environmentally friendly alternatives may not suffice if we continue to consume excessive energy. Even eco-friendly infrastructure has its own carbon footprint. Real change requires a shift in our attitudes and consumption habits. We should aim to consume below the expected energy requirements and supplement it with renewable energy sources to achieve truly environmentally conscious outcomes.

Building Sustainable Communities

Start with writing goals for the project. What is the project intending to deliver? The goals could be enhancing the quality of life and health of the occupants, protecting and restoring water resources, percentage energy reduction, protecting and enhancing biodiversity, reducing greenhouse gas emissions, promoting a sustainable lifestyle, creating a green economy, etc.

Establishing project goals holds significant importance, and it is essential for all stakeholders involved in the project to collectively arrive at and agree upon these objectives. This includes the project owner, architect, MEP consultant, sustainability consultant, landscape consultant, interior designer, contractors, engineering team, and site personnel. By involving all key stakeholders in the goal-setting process, the project can ensure alignment, collaboration, and a shared vision toward achieving sustainability and success.

The project team should establish key performance indicators for each goal to measure the performance against each goal. This will create a roadmap to achieve the sustainable goals for the project. It is ideal for locating a project within a neighborhood with existing infrastructure to reduce transportation. You could also take up barren land instead of previously fertile agricultural land or forest land to avoid endangering regional biodiversity.

Map the baselines of the region like air quality, water quality, soil health, groundwater levels, biodiversity, education, and social and economic standards of the people in the locality. These parameters have to be mapped and observed over a period of time in order to be able to understand the rate at which these factors change or evolve in the region. The primary purpose of conducting such a study is to ensure that the project does not cause any harm or degradation to the existing conditions, even if it cannot directly improve them. This study is crucial in comprehending the region's biodiversity and identifying opportunities to enhance it. You might wonder why environmentally conscious individuals should also be concerned about social welfare. Well, these aspects are interconnected and mutually reinforcing.

Conserving and preserving nature is driven by the desire to protect future generations and safeguard the well-being of the most vulnerable communities on the planet. A sustainable approach involves designing for the future and building climate resilience, all while fostering inclusiveness through collaboration with local communities. Understanding their needs, providing skill development opportunities, and creating employment prospects are integral parts of this approach. By incorporating social welfare considerations into environmental initiatives, we can create a more holistic and impactful approach to building sustainable communities.

A fantastic approach to fostering accessible and socially inclusive practices is by creating active spaces dedicated to physical well-being. Such specially designed areas provide an opportunity for open conversations, effectively addressing societal taboos and prejudices. These unique spaces encourage interaction among members of society across various dimensions, including social, financial, physical, and community aspects.

To achieve this, the community can incorporate features like cycling pathways, walking and jogging trails, promoting sustainable modes of transportation within the area. These amenities not only encourage cycling and walking but also contribute to reducing the community's carbon footprint.

Additionally, the seating and picnic areas within these active spaces can serve as excellent alternatives to air-conditioned indoor spaces for formal and informal gatherings. By providing inviting gathering spots, these areas become ideal settings for discussions, awareness programs, and fostering a sense of community connection.

Overall, creating active spaces that prioritize physical well-being presents an opportunity to promote inclusivity, social cohesion, and environmental consciousness within the community. It brings people together, encouraging them to engage in meaningful conversations while enjoying sustainable activities that benefit both individuals and the environment.

Energy Efficiency and Renewable Energy

- DEMAND REDUCTION

- ENERGY EFFICIENCY

- RENEWABLE ENERGY

The initial and most crucial step is Demand Reduction, which involves creating energy-efficient buildings that prioritize optimal daylighting, ventilation, and shading. This can be achieved through the implementation of sustainable "building envelopes." By tailoring the building envelope to suit regional conditions, thermal comfort can be attained. Strategic window sizing and shading ensure adequate daylighting while minimizing glare and facilitating natural ventilation within interior spaces. Furthermore, the choice of materials for exterior walls and roofs can provide insulation, reducing the reliance on air conditioning systems.

A well-designed building envelope will substantially reduce the energy consumption of the building.

It's crucial to acknowledge that while installing solar panels to achieve net-zero energy consumption is beneficial, we must also be mindful of the carbon footprint associated with their manufacturing and the mining of natural resources. The production of solar panels and batteries involves high energy-intensive process, contributing to greenhouse gas emissions during manufacturing and resource extraction processes. However, when evaluating the lifecycle impact, solar panels indeed outperform conventional thermal energy sources, making them a more environmentally friendly choice. Their ability to generate clean, renewable energy without emitting greenhouse gases during operation offsets the carbon emissions from manufacturing, resulting in a net reduction in greenhouse gas emissions over their entire lifecycle.

Therefore, the wisest approach is to prioritize reducing energy demand in the first place.

The second step involves focusing on the energy efficiency of the equipment. Opt for energy-efficient appliances and consider alternative passive technologies for air-conditioning, which consume less energy. Integrating automation with daylight and occupancy sensors can further reduce energy wastage.

The final step is to replace conventional energy sources with renewable energy. Hybrid systems like Solar Wind Hybrid Systems are adaptable to various climatic conditions. Embracing renewable energy plays a crucial role in decarbonizing the energy industry and mitigating the consequences of climate change. The term "carbon intensity" measures the amount of CO2 emitted per unit of energy. By transitioning to lower-carbon sources like renewables, we can reduce emissions and lessen the carbon intensity of our energy mix. Ultimately, a comprehensive approach that combines energy demand reduction, energy efficiency, and renewable energy adoption is essential for creating sustainable and environmentally conscious projects.

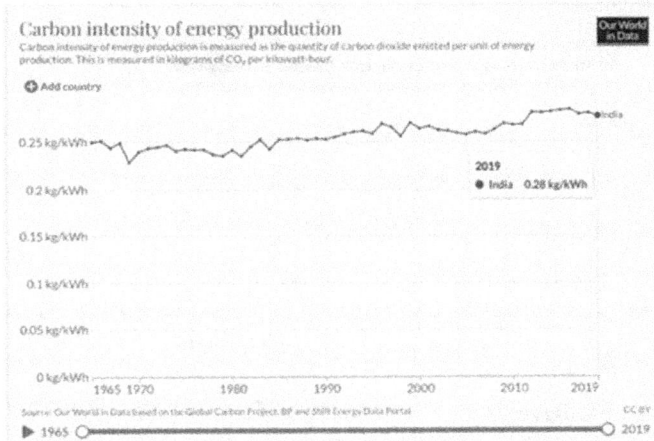

Carbon Intensity – measured in kilograms of CO2 emitted per kilogram of oil equivalent consumed.

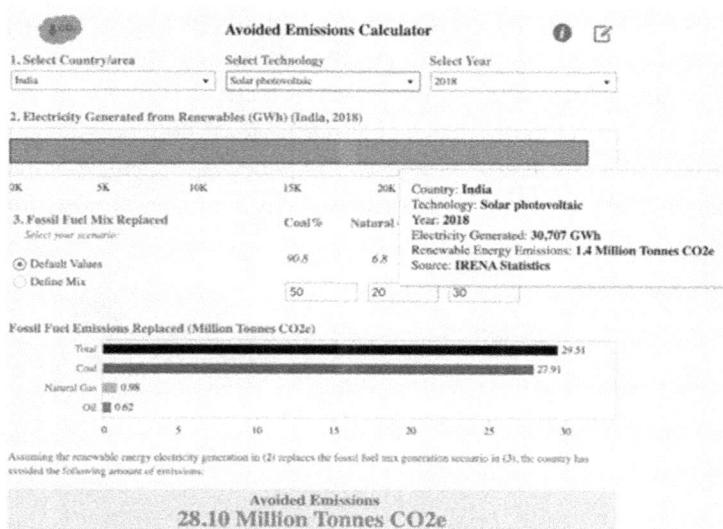

Estimated greenhouse gas emissions avoided each year as a result of renewable energy deployment for India in 2018

Water Positive

Today we are more aware than before of the consequences of water scarcity. Political analysts have also indicated that the next war could result from climate change, and water scarcity is one of its highest consequences. Thus, it is imperative to be mindful of how we consume water. Water outages are increasing as a result of the region's increased frequency of droughts, as well as the loss of several farmers' lives and livelihoods. Being water positive is the need of the hour.

Achieving water positivity in a community involves implementing strategies to ensure that the community's water consumption and usage do not deplete local water resources and, instead, contribute positively to water availability and sustainability.

Here are some steps to achieve water positivity: Water Conservation: Implement water conservation measures to reduce water wastage. This includes fixing leaks, using water-efficient fixtures and appliances, and promoting water-saving habits among residents.

1. Rainwater Harvesting: Install rainwater harvesting systems to capture and store rainwater for later use. This can supplement water needs, especially during dry periods, and reduce reliance on external water sources.
2. Wastewater treatment & Recycling: Treat and reuse wastewater from toilets for non-potable purposes such as irrigation and flushing toilets. Wastewater recycling can significantly reduce the demand for fresh water.
3. Efficient Landscaping: Design and maintain landscapes using drought-resistant plants, native species, and efficient irrigation systems to minimize water usage for landscaping purposes.
4. Sustainable Infrastructure: Incorporate sustainable design principles in buildings and infrastructure to minimize water consumption. This may include using water-efficient cooling systems, low-flow toilets, and waterless urinals.
5. Educate and Raise Awareness: Conduct educational programs and awareness campaigns to promote water conservation and responsible water use within the community.
6. Community Participation: Encourage community involvement and engagement in water conservation initiatives, fostering a sense of collective responsibility.
7. Stormwater Management: Develop effective stormwater management practices to prevent runoff and erosion, which can help recharge local groundwater sources.
8. Water Monitoring: Regularly monitor water usage and availability to identify areas for improvement and to track progress toward water positivity goals.
9. By combining these strategies and actively involving the community in water conservation efforts, it is possible to achieve water positivity, ensuring a sustainable water supply for both the current and future generations within the community.

Zero Wastewater Discharge

When wastewater is released into the environment, it contaminates the water bodies and their ecosystems. Reusing treated water reduces the demand for fresh water. Zero wastewater discharge is a wastewater management strategy to purify wastewater by subjecting it to a chain of treatments so that 90% of wastewater is recovered and recycled within the site. Thus, preventing the risk of environmental pollution associated with wastewater discharge and maximizing the efficiency of water usage, thereby striking a balance between the exploitation of freshwater resources and the preservation of the aquatic environment.

The wastewater treatment should involve natural and biological processes to ensure that the surface water is not contaminated, which minimizes the impact on local ecosystems and the climate. By treating the wastewater on-site, the burden on the local bodies to handle the sewage is reduced along with the associated costs of transport and sewage handling requirements.

Have a policy to mandate the use of natural and eco-friendly cleaning materials to reduce the flow of toxic waste into wastewater. The seepage of toxic substances into water streams kills organisms that are essential for maintaining the natural ecosystem while also making it unsafe for human consumption. Conventional chemical substances have a terrible impact on our waterways, air quality, soil health, and wildlife habitats.

Resource Efficiency

The domestic waste from communities is often dumped in landfills that are located far from the city centers - in rural areas and outskirts of the city. The negligent disposal mechanism of such waste can create toxic environments for the residents living there, in addition to soil and water pollution in the surrounding areas.

For a long time, we have depended on landfills to get rid of our trash. Population explosion, coupled with improved lifestyle needs of people, results in increased solid waste generation in urban and rural areas of the country. All waste becomes hazardous if not carefully disposed of, resulting in irreversible damage to Earth over time. But what is equally important is that all waste is recyclable.

Recycling reduces the demand for virgin materials and consumes less water and energy. There is a need to study waste not merely as an environmental polluter but as a recyclable material of great potential for saving energy.

Strategies for Waste Management and Reduction

The type and amount of garbage produced by the community should be tracked. Residents, staff, and vendors should all be trained in trash reduction.

The waste hierarchy demonstrates the most effective strategy to avert the depletion of precious resources by inhibiting waste from being generated in the first place. The goal is to maximize efficiency while avoiding wasteful consumption through actions such as:

- Choosing things with the least amount of packaging or that need the fewest resources to create.
- Avoiding the use of disposable items or single-use materials.
- Purchasing recycled, recyclable, repairable, refillable, reusable, or biodegradable products.
- Utilizing leftover food instead of throwing it away.

Types of Waste

Domestic waste can be broadly classified into 5 types:

- Dry Waste (paper, plastics, tetra packs, cardboard, glass, thermocol, etc.)
- Wet Waste (food leftovers, rotten fruits, eggshells, tea leaves, flowers, etc.)
- Sanitary Waste (sanitary napkins, diapers, bandages, condoms,

etc.)

- E-Waste (all electronic waste like batteries, phones, chargers, computer parts, appliances, etc.)
- Hazardous Waste (chemicals, cosmetics, paints, oils, medicines, syringes, razors, broken glass, etc.)

Segregation of Waste at Home Level

For simplification and ease of segregation for residents, there could be three bins right at home level:

- Dry Waste
- Wet Waste
- Reject Waste – Sanitary & Hazardous Waste

An on-site organic waste composter or a Biogas plant can be installed to handle wet waste for compost or power generation. The methane produced from the Biogas plant could be connected to a community kitchen for cooking purposes or to generate power. Dry waste could be transferred to a central waste storage facility where it will be further segregated into papers, cardboard, plastic, metals, rubber, thermocol, etc., All recyclable materials should be sent to a recycling facility, and non-recyclable plastics should be used as raw material in 'Waste to Energy' systems to recover energy. Electronic waste should be collected quarterly by the housekeeping team and stored centrally to be picked up by E-waste recycling vendors.

Hazardous waste like chemicals, paints, oils, and pesticides should be separately stored in the HHW bin at the central waste storage facility to be handed over to the permitted Hazardous waste treatment facility.

Materials

Building materials indeed consume a significant amount of energy throughout their life cycle, from raw material extraction to transportation and construction. Optimizing the embodied energy in materials is crucial for sustainability, as resource extraction activities can lead to habitat loss, land degradation, and pollution. To reduce the negative impact on the environment, minimizing the use of raw materials through reuse and recycling is highly effective. Exploring alternative materials can also help decrease reliance on virgin resources.

Several interventions can be adopted to promote sustainable material choices:

1.   Designing with Local and Recycled Materials: Using materials sourced locally reduces energy consumption related to transportation. Incorporating recycled content in building materials further reduces the need for new raw materials and lessens environmental impact.

2.   Extending the Life of Salvaged Materials: Salvaged materials can be repurposed or refurbished, providing a sustainable alternative to using new materials. This approach helps cut emissions associated with raw material extraction.

3.   FSC-Certified Wood: Opting for wood from forests certified by the Forest Stewardship Council (FSC) ensures responsible forest management practices, including protecting ecosystems, respecting indigenous cultures, and monitoring the chain of custody to guarantee sustainability.

4.   Rapidly Renewable Materials: Materials derived from rapidly renewable sources such as bamboo, cork, and natural rubber are excellent choices as they reduce reliance on fossil-fuel derivatives and contribute to sustainability.

By adopting these strategies and making mindful choices in selecting building materials, construction projects can significantly reduce their environmental impact and move towards more sustainable and eco-friendly practices.

Sustainable Food Production

Creating a portion of land within the project for the edible plantation to produce fruits and vegetables is an excellent step towards self-sufficiency and sustainability. By achieving self-reliance in fruit and vegetable production, the community can reduce food miles and enjoy the health benefits of consuming fresh, organic, and locally grown produce.

To ensure successful and efficient farming practices, comprehensive cropping patterns should be employed, taking into account the soil type and suitability for different vegetable and fruit varieties. Native tree and plant species should be prioritized to improve biodiversity, and at least 30% of diverse plant species should be introduced to promote a healthy ecosystem.

Community farming can be designed based on available water resources, and green areas can be dedicated to forests, fruits, and vegetables with diverse cropping patterns to maximize nutrient supply to the plants.

During community farming procedures, the use of natural pest control methods, such as Biocontrol Agents, Herbal Concoctions, and trap crops, should be employed to minimize the need for chemical pesticides. Vegetable waste, farm litter, and animal waste from housing units and communal spaces can be transformed into valuable compost manure through controlled anaerobic decomposition, supporting sustainable soil health and crop growth.

Incorporating animal husbandry units capable of supplying milk, meat, and eggs to the community can further enhance self-sufficiency and promote holistic sustainability practices.

By implementing these strategies and following sustainable agricultural practices, the community can not only achieve self-reliance in food production but also contribute to environmental conservation and the overall well-being of its residents.

Air Quality Control

Vehicular pollution is a major global concern that can be significantly reduced by promoting safer and more efficient commuting options, such as e-bikes, cycles, and other sustainable modes of transportation. The project should prioritize landscaping and afforestation activities that are chemical-free, ensuring zero exposure to pesticides for the end-users.

Indoor air quality is equally important, considering that people spend more than 90% of their time indoors, either at home or work. Indoor environments can have pollutant concentrations 2 to 5 times higher than outdoor levels due to inadequate ventilation and the use of synthetic construction materials, furnishings, personal care items, pesticides, and home cleaners.

Volatile organic compounds (VOCs) play a significant role in ground-level ozone generation and are critical indoor pollutants. When VOCs combine with nitrogen oxides (NOx), they form ozone molecules, contributing to smog and negatively impacting human health. To mitigate these risks and ensure the well-being of inhabitants, it's essential to choose products with low VOC content, known as low VOC products. Opting for such products will reduce the emission of harmful compounds into indoor air and improve overall indoor air quality.

By addressing vehicular pollution, adopting chemical-free landscaping practices, and promoting low VOC products, the project can contribute to a healthier and more sustainable living environment for its residents, reducing both outdoor and indoor pollution.

Monitoring Operational Performance

A significant portion of a building's energy use occurs during the operational stage, typically accounting for 80-90% of its total energy consumption over its lifetime. This operational stage encompasses the day-to-day activities and functions of the building, including heating, cooling, lighting, ventilation, hot water supply, electrical appliances, and other systems used by its occupants.

Life Cycle Energy Use of Buildings (%)

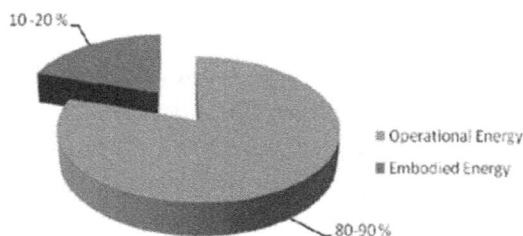

While the initial design and construction of a building may prioritize sustainability, its long-term sustainability can only be achieved if it is responsibly operated and maintained. Building operations and maintenance (O&M) employees play a crucial role in ensuring the building's ongoing viability and eco-friendliness.

Proactive O&M practices are essential for maximizing the building's sustainability. When O&M teams operate proactively rather than reactively, they can identify potential issues early on and implement preventive maintenance measures. This approach helps to avoid emergency repairs and ensures smooth facility management at all levels.

Having a real-time view of the operational state of various building components, such as Mechanical, Electrical, Environmental, and Plumbing systems, is instrumental in achieving proactive maintenance. This visibility allows O&M teams to monitor and assess the building's performance continuously, enabling them to take timely actions and address potential concerns before they escalate.

However, one significant challenge in achieving green construction techniques is the lack of visibility into operational data. Access to real-time data and analytics can significantly enhance the building's energy efficiency and sustainability. By leveraging technology and data-driven insights, O&M personnel can make informed decisions and optimize the building's performance over time.

The Need to Correct the Existing Building Infrastructure

The built environment in cities accounts for 75% of annual worldwide greenhouse gas emissions. With global energy consumption increasing, it is critical to develop energy-saving solutions. Because old buildings consume a large portion of a country's energy (40% of energy consumption in the US can be attributed to buildings, and commercial buildings account for 18% of UK carbon emissions), it's prudent to consider them as potential avenues of improvement in order to reduce carbon emissions.

More than 220 million existing buildings in Europe alone are energy-inefficient, accounting for 75% of the building stock, with many reliant on fossil fuels for heating and cooling. According to our System Value Initiative's European analysis, a 20% shift in heating toward heat pump applications powered by renewable electricity would reduce CO_2 emissions by 9%. When combined with smart solutions, it has the potential to save €3 billion in human health benefits from reduced air pollution between now and 2030. Remember that any building built today will be around for the next 50 years or more, so ensuring that new buildings are green and existing buildings are decarbonized is critical to our efforts to battle climate change.

The problem with existing buildings is that they are already built, they have embodied energy, and they are further consuming more energy in their operation due to inefficient envelopes, equipment, and systems. How do we reduce the carbon footprint or energy utilization of an old building? Bringing the building down and building a new one with green principles is not a sustainable option. We could look at retrofitting the existing buildings with efficient systems and automation that can allow it to perform better and consume less energy and resources. Deploy a strategy to determine the best options for energy and sustainability improvements.

- Conduct a Water Audit to assess the operation of the building's water systems because leaking and inefficient systems not only wastewater but also squander energy by running pumps and other electrical equipment inefficiently.

- Examine utility bills from the last two years to see if use has increased.
- Examine the building envelope for leaky windows, gaps around vents and pipe penetrations, and moisture intrusion to determine the air tightness of the building envelope. Upgrading heating and cooling systems without addressing building envelope issues will result in less-than-optimal system performance.
- Install daylighting and occupancy sensors in appropriate locations. Incorporate energy-efficient lighting into the project.
- Determine whether natural ventilation and fresh air intake are viable options for reducing heating and cooling loads.
- Examine renewable energy choices that can be used to offset the purchase of fossil-fuel-based energy.
- Replace old windows with high-performance windows that are temperature and exposure-appropriate.
- Consider the benefits of distributed generation if the building is part of a campus cluster or can share the on-site energy produced with neighbouring buildings.
- A cool roof or green roof can be installed to reduce the heat island effects.
- Make use of the opportunity provided by the building renovation to implement sustainable operations and maintenance practices, as well as to convert to green cleaning products and procedures.
- Measure the performance of a freshly renovated facility on a regular basis to ensure it continues to perform as intended.
- Consider metering all key energy-consuming devices. Smart meters and submeters are preferred for monitoring real-time use, controlling demand, and controlling costs.
- Before contemplating replacing current equipment with newer, higher-efficiency equipment, conduct an energy audit to see whether the existing systems are running at peak efficiency. Evaluation of the performance of the building envelope and

existing systems can sometimes result in significant savings in utility costs: leaks, clogged/dirty filters, stuck dampers, disabled sensors, faulty or incorrect wiring, or even a lack of knowledge on how to properly operate and maintain equipment can all contribute to inefficiencies and increased costs.

Net Zero Projects

A net-zero project refers to an initiative or undertaking that aims to achieve net-zero greenhouse gas (GHG) emissions. The term "net zero" means that the project's overall carbon or GHG emissions are balanced by removing an equivalent amount of emissions from the atmosphere or by offsetting those emissions through various means.

The concept of net zero is an essential component of climate change mitigation efforts, as it contributes to reducing the overall impact of human activities on the environment. Achieving net-zero emissions is critical in combating global warming and limiting the rise in average global temperatures.

To become a net-zero project, several key steps are typically involved:

Emissions Reduction: The project aims to minimize carbon or GHG emissions at the source through energy-efficient technologies, cleaner production methods, and sustainable practices.

Renewable Energy: Net-zero projects often focus on generating energy from renewable sources, such as solar, wind, hydro, or geothermal, to replace or reduce reliance on fossil fuels.

Carbon Offsetting: If the project cannot completely eliminate all emissions, it can invest in carbon offsetting initiatives. Carbon offsetting involves supporting activities that remove or reduce emissions elsewhere, like reforestation, afforestation, or investing in carbon capture and storage (CCS) projects.

Sustainable Practices: Implementing sustainable practices and using environmentally friendly materials throughout the project's lifecycle can help reduce its overall environmental impact.

Carbon Accounting: To become net-zero, the project needs to accurately measure and account for its emissions, including both direct emissions (Scope 1) and indirect emissions from energy consumption (Scope 2) and other sources in the supply chain (Scope 3).

Engagement and Collaboration: Successful net-zero projects often involve collaboration with stakeholders, communities, and partners to gain support and maximize impact.

The concept of net zero extends beyond individual projects and applies to broader scopes, such as net-zero cities, net-zero companies, and even net-zero countries. Governments, organizations, and businesses around the world are increasingly committing to achieving net-zero emissions in their operations and activities to combat climate change effectively.

Sponge Cities

There is an urgency to address climate change and the need for sustainable urban planning. "Sponge cities" are indeed a promising approach to mitigating the impact of climate change and building more resilient cities. These cities are designed to mimic natural ecosystems and incorporate features that help absorb, retain, and manage water in a sustainable manner, reducing the risk of flooding and improving water quality.

As you mentioned, China has been at the forefront of implementing sponge city initiatives, especially in response to the increasing challenges of urbanization and climate change. By integrating green spaces, permeable pavements, green roofs, and other nature-based solutions, sponge cities can absorb rainwater and reduce the burden on traditional drainage systems during heavy rainfall events.

Singapore's efforts to become a "garden city" also demonstrate the positive impact of incorporating greenery into urban environments. The city's focus on green spaces not only enhances the aesthetics but also provides numerous environmental benefits, such as mitigating the urban heat island effect, improving air quality, and supporting biodiversity.

Implementing sponge city concepts and investing in nature-based solutions is crucial for urban areas worldwide, as climate change leads to more frequent and intense weather events. Sustainable urban planning can help reduce the risk of flooding, support water conservation, and promote overall environmental well-being.

Vertical Forests

Vertical forests have emerged as a remarkable and innovative solution to address the challenges posed by rapid urbanization and deforestation. As cities continue to expand and natural spaces are encroached upon, finding ways to integrate nature into urban environments becomes crucial for the well-being of both residents and the environment.

The concept of vertical forests was popularized by Italian architect Stefano Boeri, who designed the Bosco Verticale (Vertical Forest) in Milan, Italy. This pioneering project features high-rise residential buildings adorned with a vast number of trees, shrubs, and plants on their balconies and facades. This forest actually boasts of flora that would otherwise occupy more than three and a half football stadiums. The lush vegetation not only enhances the visual appeal of the buildings but also provides a range of ecological benefits.

Due to the success of the Bosco Verticale in Milan, similar projects have been initiated in other cities, including those in Switzerland, the Netherlands, and China, among others. This global adoption demonstrates the increasing awareness and commitment to sustainable urban development and the integration of nature into cityscapes.

Vertical forests serve as inspiring examples of how we can blend modern architecture with environmental consciousness to create livable, healthy, and ecologically sustainable urban spaces. As more such initiatives are undertaken, they can contribute to a greener, more resilient future for our urban landscapes. However, it's essential to continue exploring and implementing a variety of sustainable practices and policies to tackle the complex challenges of urbanization and environmental degradation effectively.

Twenty-Minute Neighborhoods

The vision of having all essential amenities within a 20-minute walking distance from our homes holds the promise of saving significant energy and time. In bustling cities like Mumbai, where the pace of life is fast, distances are often measured in time rather than meters. This concept has inspired city planners to design communities where residents can easily access businesses, local markets, and workplaces within a mere 20-minute walk from their homes, thus reducing the reliance on public transport. Many cities in the developed world have already embraced this way of life, recognizing its numerous benefits.

Paris, for instance, is at the forefront of adopting the 15-minute city model, striving to create neighborhoods where residents can meet all their needs within a short 15-minute walk. By adopting this approach, cities aim to promote convenience, efficiency, and sustainability. The concept encourages a more active lifestyle, reduces environmental impacts, and fosters a sense of community by emphasizing local businesses and services.

As this idea gains momentum, it presents an exciting vision for the future of urban planning and livable cities. By bringing amenities closer to people's homes, we can create more inclusive and accessible environments that enhance the overall well-being of residents. This approach not only reduces the burden of commuting but also creates vibrant and interconnected communities, fostering a stronger sense of belonging and quality of life. As more cities embrace this way of life, we move closer to achieving greener, more people-centric urban spaces that prioritize efficiency, sustainability, and the overall happiness of their inhabitants.

Mini Urban Forests

As a civilization, it is essential for us to reverse the detrimental effects of unregulated deforestation and prioritize reforestation and nature integration in our urban areas. Historically, we cleared forests to build our cities, but now we must recognize the importance of green spaces for the environment and human well-being.

The concept of building miniature forests within cities, inspired by Japanese temples, is a fantastic approach to addressing the challenges posed by climate change and habitat loss. These miniature forests can consist of a diverse range of native flora, which not only promotes biodiversity but also offers a multitude of environmental benefits.

By intermingling tiny yet dense forests within urban landscapes, we can create pockets of nature that serve as havens for both people and wildlife. These green oases offer an opportunity to reconnect with nature while making cities more resilient to the challenges of climate change.

Smart Commutation

The realization of the benefits of public transportation and the growing awareness of the importance of green spaces have spurred regeneration projects in cities worldwide. These initiatives are transforming previously unused or neglected areas into vibrant green parks, providing much-needed recreational spaces for urban dwellers.

Bangkok, like many other cities, has embraced such regeneration projects, repurposing old railway tracks and other underutilized plots into new green parks. This not only enhances the city's aesthetics but also contributes to the overall well-being of its inhabitants. Green spaces offer a respite from the concrete jungle, allowing people to connect with nature and enjoy a healthier and more sustainable urban environment.

As these regeneration projects become more prevalent, they shape the perception of what makes a good city, prompting more individuals and communities to take part in building their own green initiatives. Citizens are becoming proactive in creating green spaces, community gardens, and urban farms, further contributing to the transformation of urban landscapes.

Advancements in technology have also played a significant role in promoting sustainable urban living. The development of apps that assist in discovering the most efficient public transportation routes reflects the growing emphasis on eco-friendly travel options. By using these digital tools, people can make informed decisions about their travel routes, reducing congestion and carbon emissions in cities.

With the majority of the global population projected to live in urban areas by 2050, finding effective solutions to combat climate change becomes imperative for ensuring habitable and sustainable cities. By prioritizing public transportation, green infrastructure, and sustainable urban planning, cities can mitigate the impacts of climate change, reduce pollution, and create more livable environments for their residents.

Sustainable Projects Across The World

Organo Naandi

Organo Naandi is a remarkable example of an eco-friendly and sustainable farming community located in Hyderabad, India. Conceived by visionary architects, this community consists of 73 villas designed to coexist and share resources as a close-knit community.

The primary goal of Organo Naandi is to counter the effects of widespread urbanization and give back to nature by creating a harmonious living space that encourages a healthy and environmentally friendly lifestyle. The community offers a unique blend of rural and urban experiences, providing its residents with a well-balanced and sustainable way of living.

One of the key features of the project is its self-sufficiency in energy and water resources. The community generates its own power and even exports excess power to the grid. They rely solely on rainwater and groundwater, which is captured and managed through a well-designed stormwater network consisting of trenches, swales, ponds, and deep aquifer recharge systems.

To ensure comfortable living without excessive reliance on conventional cooling systems, Organo Naandi employs passive cooling technology known as Earth Air Tunnel Draft. This technology helps reduce the need for HVAC (Heating, Ventilation, and Air Conditioning) cooling while also providing fresh air ventilation for the villas.

Food production is another significant aspect of Organo Naandi's sustainability efforts. The community produces organically grown fruits and vegetables, and milk is sourced from their own cattle farm (Goshala) to meet the dietary requirements sustainably and locally. This focus on organic farming not only promotes a healthier lifestyle for the residents but also contributes to the preservation of the environment.

The commendable efforts put forth by Organo Naandi have gained recognition on a global scale. In 2018, the initiative was honored with the Leadership in Sustainable Design and Performance award by the World Green Building Council. Additionally, the collaboration with BBC Story Works on the TV show titled 'Building a Better Future' has brought further attention to this exemplary project.

Organo Naandi serves as a model for sustainable communities that prioritize ecological balance, resource efficiency, and responsible living. By demonstrating the possibilities of such eco-habitats, this project inspires and encourages the adoption of sustainable practices in future urban and rural developments.

Catskills Project

The Catskills project in New York has gained global recognition for its innovative approach to establishing a sustainable and carbon-neutral community. Situated on 90 acres of land in Livingston Manor, this community showcases the seamless integration of passive house design and efficient infrastructure to create environmentally friendly homes that cater to the needs of both residents and nature.

The project's emphasis on craftsmanship and quality ensures that the homes are not only eco-friendly but also offer a high standard of living for their inhabitants. To achieve its net-zero goals, the community utilizes panelized wall systems, carbon tracking features, and renewable energy sources, including affordable solar infrastructure, to power the houses.

Led by the visionary architect Buck Moorhead, the team behind the Catskills project carefully researches and selects materials that align with their environmentally conscious approach. By avoiding high embodied energy materials like steel and concrete, which require substantial resources for production and transportation, the team has successfully minimized the project's environmental impact.

Instead, the houses are constructed primarily with wood and upcycled materials, providing a sustainable and easily reusable alternative. The integration of thermal bridges also prevents heat loss from the interiors, contributing to the community's energy efficiency.

The implementation of solar panels in each home has significantly reduced the community's annual energy requirements, further reinforcing its commitment to carbon neutrality.

Although some critics have expressed concerns about repurposing rural land for luxury homes, the project's creators stress their intention to coexist harmoniously with the environment. The site was thoughtfully chosen to preserve the existing forest cover and minimize the project's impact on the natural surroundings.

By setting a benchmark for sustainable housing and community development, the Catskills project serves as an inspiring example of how we can build homes that prioritize the well-being of residents and the planet. It showcases that with innovative design, responsible material choices, and renewable energy solutions, it is possible to create living spaces that contribute positively to the environment while meeting the needs of modern-day living.

Tree House, Singapore

Tree House is an architectural masterpiece inspired not just by its surroundings, which are mostly a green oasis, but also by Biomimicry or nature-inspired innovation. The Tree House concept aspires to enhance this situation, to sync with its natural surroundings and give the same within the built world. By researching current biodiversity and climatic conditions, site planning embraces the natural environment. The development was subjected to a Biodiversity Impact Assessment (BIA) to maintain the continuation of the native environment, vertical greenery, and abundant landscaping.

The spectacular and majestic 24-story-high Green Wall in Tree House was built to provide "vertical" continuity of greenery from nearby "horizontal" green surrounds, as well as to function as a Bio-shield to maximize green lungs and reduce solar radiation and cooling burden. The Bio-shield is roughly 24 floors tall (78 meters) and 20 meters wide. Green sky gardens on the 7th, 13th, and 19th floors of each building complement the nature-inspired architecture, with green creepers gripped on the circular support. Residents can use these as vantage spots and additional vertical green lungs. The vast cantilever of sky gardens optimizes vegetation and offers shade for Tree House's interior rooms.

To make use of passive environmental design, conventional lobbies, and subterranean parking garages were constructed to be naturally ventilated, fulfilling the need for mechanical ventilation, smoke purging, and sprinkler systems. Such thought has had a considerable impact on the natural daylight delivered into the basement, as well as the necessity for mechanical ventilation. This has allowed the homeowner to benefit from natural lighting and ventilation throughout the day. The development's design and construction, with careful consideration of passive design and the use of sustainable materials, improve energy and water efficiency to achieve a higher level of interior environmental quality.

Because the land parcel is undulating, the landscape deck and basement design were tiered to accommodate the site's existing sloping levels. The method reduced Earth-cutting during excavation, lowering the environmental impact on the site. The development also made use of a Cobiax flooring system. A void-forming system that forms lightweight, biaxial floor slabs, reducing the volume of concrete by displacing non-working dead load and lowering foundation costs. Tree House, an eco-inspired residential building, has established new sustainability benchmarks and defined a new age of living in harmony with nature in a densely populated urban area such as Singapore.

ZCB, Hong Kong

The Construction Industry Council (CIC) and the government of Hong Kong collaborated to develop ZCB (Zero Carbon Building), the first of its kind in the city, with the aim of showcasing cutting-edge eco-building design and technology. Given that Hong Kong's buildings account for 89% of the total electricity consumption, ZCB was purposefully designed to address the unique challenges of the high-density, hot, and humid sub-tropical urban context.

The building's adaptable design allows it to switch between a

tightly sealed, air-conditioned environment and a highly porous, cross-ventilated space, depending on the needs and weather conditions. Synergistic design and building systems work together to deliver high environmental quality and performance.

To minimize cooling loads during peak summer periods, ZCB features a large open plan and cross-ventilated layout, along with a high-performance building envelope incorporating Low-E insulated glass units and deep overhangs. Natural ventilation and high-volume, low-speed fans are employed during non-peak times to counter humid weather.

ZCB takes a holistic approach to sustainability by mitigating the local heat island effect and harnessing solar and urban wind energy. Over 1,000 building-integrated solar photovoltaics have been incorporated into the building fabric, allowing ZCB to generate enough renewable energy for its own operation and even export surplus energy back to the grid. Over its 50-year lifespan, the building is expected to reduce carbon emissions by 7,100 tons.

The building is equipped with more than 2,800 sensing points, including four microclimate stations, which monitor six dimensions of building performance. This information is shared with occupants and visitors through interactive, real-time displays, promoting awareness and engagement with sustainable practices.

Open to the public, ZCB serves as an educational and demonstration platform. It is expected to attract around 40,000 visitors annually for tours, seminars, conferences, and other events, including eco-weddings. Within its premises, ZCB houses a green office for the CIC, a demonstration home for low-carbon living, a multifunction room, and Hong Kong's first urban native woodland. The high greenery coverage, which comprises half of the site, not only enhances biodiversity and amenity but also provides shade, cooling the building during the hot summer months.

An interesting cultural aspect of ZCB is the implementation of a 'cool biz dress code,' fostering a cultural shift towards sustainable living. By setting a world-class example of a low-carbon, highly energy-efficient building, ZCB acts as a living laboratory for sustainability, providing a valuable learning and teaching tool for the community.

Final Thoughts

The COVID-19 pandemic has indeed brought to light the limitations and drawbacks of urban living, prompting a desire for more open and naturally vibrant spaces. Many urban communities are grappling with destructive lifestyles that have adverse impacts on both the planet and human health. The urgent need of the hour is to shift towards building sustainable communities that prioritize environmental responsibility and overall well-being.

A sustainable community comprises individuals who are well aware of the economic, social, and political consequences of climate change. They are proactive in collaborating with each other to develop and implement sustainable practices that can be seamlessly integrated into everyday life.

Working in partnership with local governments, political units, and residents, sustainable communities focus on various crucial aspects. They strive to establish water-positive systems, ensuring that water resources are conserved and efficiently utilized. This includes rainwater harvesting and responsible water management practices.

Sustainable communities also prioritize waste reduction and management, aiming to eliminate landfills and promote recycling and composting to minimize waste generation.

To combat air pollution, these communities actively engage in initiatives to reduce emissions, such as promoting alternative transportation options, supporting clean energy sources, and implementing green building practices.

Moreover, sustainable communities encourage and incentivize the adoption of net-zero energy solutions, wherein the energy consumed is offset by renewable energy generation. This approach not only reduces the environmental impact but also contributes to energy independence and resilience.

Education and awareness play a crucial role in building sustainable communities, as individuals need to understand the significance of their actions and choices in shaping a greener future.

By collectively working towards creating sustainable communities, we can address the pressing environmental challenges we face today and secure a better, more resilient future for generations to come. It requires a joint effort from individuals, local authorities, and policymakers to foster a shared commitment to environmental stewardship and a more balanced and harmonious way of life.

6

MINIMALISM

"The secret of happiness is not found in seeking more, but in developing the capacity to enjoy less."

- Socrates

A look around us reveals that we have more than what we need to sustain ourselves. Over the years, innovation and creativity have served a wide variety of purposes. In the old days, we used innovative products to increase the speed and efficiency with which our day-to-day tasks were completed. Today, a lot of the material objects that surround us serve to meet more than our utilitarian needs. We purchase home decor items for aesthetic pleasure, wish to purchase bigger houses with more rooms that can accommodate our guests comfortably, and we wish to live in gated communities that come with their own set of outdoor resources like swimming pools and clubs, and so much more. Truly, we have maximized the scale at which we live, especially when it comes to the material objects we depend upon in our lives. A toaster tends to do a better job than a pan for us; in the same kitchen - one is likely to find a toaster oven, a baking oven, and a microwave - all similar yet unique in a few ways. However, it is not new information that our reliance on a materialistic lifestyle is dangerous for the environment.

The world began to realize the futility of a lifestyle that is driven by material pleasures. As an answer to this, several people have begun to practice a "minimalist" lifestyle. This new philosophical intervention in the way we live and consume resources has been welcomed by people all across the world. People are researching minimalist interventions that can be brought to the many professions of the world so that we as a civilization may rely on material objects a lot less than we do. This would involve not just the need to shed dependability on resources but also an efficient use of the resources we choose to continue using in our lives.

What is Minimalism?

Minimalism is a concept that has taken over the world by storm. It is the subject of documentaries, lifestyle bloggers, and so much more. In fact, over the years, this lifestyle choice has made its way into several prominent industries of the world, such as - fashion, design, food, housing, beauty, and more. Despite its popularity in the market, we consumers often fail to understand the concept and its message. Traditionally, Minimalism has been equated with a concept from art and design. In essence, it is the process of identifying what is essential to our lives, and in return, we must eliminate what is not. When we declutter our lives by removing the unwanted, we can find ourselves with more time and energy. Thus, this is a lifestyle choice born out of the saying "less is more." What was once an elitist idea that was meant to signify "class" has now blown up as an entire way of life! Truly, what an astounding reminder that in the end, after all our efforts on the planet to become successful, we must now move to a reductive lifestyle in order to survive. At the moment, most of us tend to live a maximalist lifestyle. We wish to replace our phones with the latest model; our clothes must match the latest trends as well. Likewise, furniture has undoubtedly become a victim of trends as well - so much so that we are willing to compromise on the comfort and longevity of a product only if it can match the aesthetic of our dreams. Thus, as a result of such an overwhelming life, we often find ourselves distracted by physical, digital, and mental preoccupations.

This has led to increased anxiety and a chronic sense of dissatisfaction with life. In a bid to distract ourselves from the present, we keep finding materialistic objects to hook onto. Scientific research has indicated that a cluttered lifestyle can elevate our stress levels which in turn can reduce our focus drastically. This, in turn, reduces the time we can devote to our loved ones for exercise, cooking healthy food, or just taking a good rest after a hectic day. Of course, this negligence is taking a toll on our mental and physical health.

What Are the Benefits of a Minimalist Approach to Life?

We often associate excess of something with a higher status, sense of security, and comfort. We assume that our friends and peers who seem to have "more" are in control of their lives, leading a much easier life than we are. However, this is simply not true. How can having more make us stress-free? The more we have, the more there is to lessen. It is a secret known to all that a simple life has its merits because of the comfort of efficiency and trust.

When we live "small," we have the unique opportunity to explore life more deeply. It helps us become nimble, flexible, and agile. Simply put - a minimalist lifestyle can help us curb whatever trouble life hurls at us. Our senses get quicker at responding to changes, making day-to-day hassles a lot less worrisome than before. The lack of things gives us fewer responsibilities to take care of, making space for a richer experience of life. The constraints of a minimalist lifestyle can help us in creating an innovative approach to life - leading to helpful breakthroughs. Most importantly, living a small life can allow you to take more risks. A minimalist lifestyle is a perfect alternative to the competitive life we have found ourselves shrouded in.

Many people who have opted for a minimalist lifestyle have advocated dropping private vehicles from their life. Growing up, we all thought of cars and houses as an inevitable part of our future. We aspire to have well-paying jobs that can help us buy our own cars and houses that can ensure an independent life for us all. However, statistics from the changing environment indicate a different story altogether.

Cars have become one of the largest sources of pollution in the world. In India, we have seen how cities like Delhi had to initiate the odd-even policy to reduce traffic on the road. This initiative became inevitable because of the rise of air pollution in the city. Moreover, public transport is a healthy and versatile alternative to private vehicles. They are known to be more efficient, quicker, and cheaper. With public transport, a family of four can be at four different places at once because they do not need to depend upon their one private vehicle. People who have switched to public transportation entirely have also spoken about how it can open the window to new experiences. Taking the local bus for work or walking short distances instead of taking a car can make us more mindful of our surroundings. Just try and think. Think about it, when was the last time you stopped to think about the name of the beautiful tree near your office or pondered about the new cafe near your home?

A minimalist lifestyle offers a break from our confined and individualistic life, opening up avenues for community-driven events that are eco-friendly in nature.

What Are the Misconceptions Around Minimalism?

Minimalism has garnered a significant number of admirers who appreciate its principles and benefits. However, it has not been immune to criticism from naysayers. While some may question the practicality or feasibility of Minimalism in their own lives, others may dismiss it as a mere trend or label it as an extreme lifestyle choice. The idea of owning fewer possessions or prioritizing experiences over material possessions may be met with resistance or skepticism by those who hold different values or attachments to consumerism. Nonetheless, despite the criticism, Minimalism continues to resonate with many individuals who seek a simpler, more intentional way of living.

Several people believe that Minimalism is a way of life that expects us to discard everything we own. Of course not! We aren't monks, and no one can pull us apart from our favorite coffee mug or pair of jeans. We are human beings; after all, we need these things for our survival. Instead of getting rid of everything you own, Minimalism wishes for you to rediscover your likes and stick to them. It encourages getting rid of things that cause stress and chaos. Moreover, a minimalist lifestyle will enable you to replace things for a better experience instead of adding to a pile of unused items.

It is essential to understand that Minimalism is not a concept that can be adopted and changed quickly. It will take time to cultivate new ways of being. The time it takes to find your path may be longer or shorter - it can vary according to your situation. It is believed that a gradual transformation is the best way to switch to a purposeful life. Furthermore, Minimalism is often fashioned as a quantitative lifestyle. There are several clickbait lifestyle videos that encourage living with "50 items only" or any such number. Of course, this is not a competition! If you wish to adopt a minimalist lifestyle, you need not succumb to the pressure of owning less than someone else. Your approach to a purposeful life will be different from someone else's. As long as you get to have the things you need to live happily and satisfactorily, you're good.

A minimalist is often confused with a stoic. No, minimalists are not emotionless robots. People find a minimalist lifestyle cold and heartless because they believe that it demands us to get rid of items of sentimental value in our lives. Instead, most minimalists have been found to be rather sentimental. They ascribe value to things that may otherwise not have much financial value.

Moreover, material objects are not the only way we can treasure our memories. We live with them, and often, they can alter our perceptions as well. Thus, a clutter-free life does not need to be devoid of emotions and sentiment - rather, it can help us manage our emotions so that we can focus on what is important to us and get rid of waste. Lastly, many people believe that Minimalism is temporary in nature, that it is just a phase of life and cannot be practiced at all times. However, one must understand that a minimalist lifestyle is not a cheat code to short-term happiness. It is a mindset, a way of life and thought. Regardless of where you live, who you live with, and what kind of work you do - once you embrace the world of Minimalism, you will carry those values with you wherever you are. What's more, you get to develop your own style and aesthetic. Your clear sense of purpose will help you make decisions; hence, you will have the time and energy to develop your surroundings just how you like them.

Everyone needs to understand that if we let go of things that don't matter; we are free to do things that really matter. If there is a lot of unnecessary stuff in the house, it takes a lot of time and money to clean and maintain them. Minimalism is not getting rid of everything. Letting go doesn't mean throwing all the stuff that you don't need. The world cannot handle that amount of trash.

A minimalist lifestyle offers you the unique experience of having deeper community experiences as well as a more soulful relationship with the self. It gives us the time and energy to concentrate and figure out what we really need. A minimalist lifestyle can help one overcome the shackles of consumerism and materialistic distractions.

The key to a minimalist lifestyle is this: decide what you want to accomplish, not what other people want you to. Once you open up to the idea of reducing intake, you can escape the trend train. Consider how liberating it would be to no longer be concerned with mainstream advice. Instead, you may create a timeless experience.

Housing Crisis

Real estate is at an all-time high in India. Cities like Mumbai continue to be unaffordable to those who do not own property here. According to an Economic Times report, Delhi NCR builders will need six years to sell more than 1.01 lakh unsold housing stocks, whereas Bengaluru will need only 31 months. Higher demand for housing has led to a decrease in "inventory hang." This inventory hang refers to the time period that builders take to sell unsold stock on the basis of sales velocity. A decline in the inventory hang indicates a higher demand for housing. Thus, as per the report, Delhi NCR has the highest inventory hang, and Bengaluru has the lowest. According to the real estate consultant Anarock, housing sales have increased by up to 71% in January and March across cities like Delhi NCR, Mumbai Metropolitan Region, Pune, Chennai, Kolkata, Hyderabad, and Bengaluru. This begs us to ask the question - will we eventually outnumber the houses we have to live in?

A paradox for countries like India is that despite housing shortages, India has a high number of vacant houses. According to a survey, there are currently almost 11.09 million urban unoccupied residences in the country's ten states and union territories, as reported in a study by Khaitan and Co, titled "The Rental Housing Market in India." At 19%, Maharashtra has the highest number of vacant houses, followed by Gujarat and Uttar Pradesh. On the basis of cities, Gurugram has more than 25% empty houses! Mumbai and Pune have a staggering amount of empty housing as well (15 and 22%, respectively). Overall, as per the census report of 2011, more than 25 million houses out of 311 million are vacant in India. What do we make of this shocking paradox?

Looking at the data, a few questions keep hanging about. What drives individuals to purchase beyond necessity and perpetuate an unrealistic demand for constant growth? When did the notion of accumulating possessions evolve into a status symbol? It appears that many hold the misguided belief that ownership equates to happiness. However, true contentment lies in possessing items with purpose rather than striving to impress others and accruing debt.

We also maintain a certain lifestyle out of peer pressure. We don't want our children to believe that we aren't giving them things that other children have. When I was a child and until I was in college, it didn't matter to me where I was living, whether we stayed in our own house or a rented one. When I started working and got married, I thought of owning a house. We bought a 2BHK flat. After a few years, I began to think that this house was not sufficient for my growing family. We started looking for a 3BHK house. After we moved to a 3BHK house, I thought it would be good to own a piece of land where I could build my dream farmhouse in the future and then a second home as security for my kids. Then one day, I realized that I was never going to be happy even if I had four houses because there is no end to greed. This is what most of us are doing. We are not just owning things for ourselves. We keep buying more than one as an investment to secure our kids' futures. This is creating an unrealistic demand. What if instead of buying two houses now, my kid grows up and buys a house after 20 years for herself? The resources that are needed to build an additional house would wait till the next 20 years, and it will also stop the over-exploitation of the resources.

The Earth will have time to regenerate the resources. We are not completely at fault for this behavior of investing in properties as future security.

This generation has seen two major recessions and a pandemic when the majority of the population was hit hard financially. So many are putting their savings into real estate, hoping for great returns which will save them during a low period. However, this is the case for the upper middle class and elite population, who are eventually the highest contributors to climate change. The poor have the lowest environmental footprint while also being most vulnerable to climate change.

What if everyone lives like a tenant in their lifespan, just like other animals or creatures? We are here on Earth for a brief period of time. Is there a need to possess so much property which we cannot enjoy in our lifetime? Through a minimalist approach, we can help curb the widening gap between the housing shortage and vacant housing in the country. The current vacant stock has the ability to house as many as 50 million people in the country - giving shelter to more than 13% of the current urban population. More importantly, if we do not address this issue, the gap between vacancy and shortage will increase further. Trends indicate that the number of vacant houses in the country increased drastically between the 1970s and 2010s, owing to the expansion of real estate in urban regions. Adults spend a lot of time collecting the money required to buy a piece of land. This time and money could instead be utilized for a laid-back approach toward life. Through a surge in renting houses, millennials have already shown that their priorities are shifting from the allure of stability towards the need for living in the moment.

Auroville - A Case In Point

I visited Auroville a few years ago. Auroville is a name that translates to "city of dawn." It is an experimental township located in the Villupuram district of Tamil Nadu. Some parts of the township are also a part of the Union Territory of Pondicherry in India. This unique township was founded by Mirra Alfassa in the year 1968, and it was designed by Roger Anger.

The township works on the principles of Sri Aurobindo, a philosopher who believed that humans are "transitional beings." The township aims to bring like-minded people together and build a world that is devoid of discrimination and chaos. In a public message, Alfassa mentioned that –

"Auroville wants to be a universal town where men and women of all countries are able to live in peace and progressive harmony, above all creeds, all politics, and all nationalities. The purpose of Auroville is to realize human unity."

I was surprised when I heard that no one could possess any property or assets in Auroville. It is unacceptable to occupy land and buildings or participate in commercial activities within Auroville. Township, for the purpose of making a profit.

The collective property of the township is used to promote good and charitable purposes. Finances and assets are held by the trustees in trust for the members of the township and for the benefit of the entire society. If all of the population had to live in a community like this, how would the same me who wants to save for the worst day behave? I can still save money without building unnecessarily. If there was a policy that doesn't allow people to possess property, it would take out the pressure of owning a house and related stress. This would, in return, reduce the need to earn more and pay EMIs. Financial freedom comes from owning less and not from earning more.

Moreover, the material conditions of the township will be dynamic in nature and change according to the changing realizations of the community. What a wonderful goal to work with! Just like the minimalist philosophy, the manifesto for Auroville understands and celebrates the dynamic nature of human will. The way we perceive the world is constantly changing. In such a world, it is criminal to believe that we shall have singular plans that we shall never deter from. Moreover, an endless free will where we think of no one except ourselves could lead to devastation unlike any other.

Hence, the best way to live would be to understand that we are part of a community. If we find people with a similar outlook on life, we can collaborate to build a sustainable and kind world. In addition to these psychological needs, there are new rules for the material world as well.

Take care of yourself. Your spending will depend on your lifestyle and on what works for you. Free yourself of unnecessary things. You may not be a great admirer of a gadget, but if you enjoy the medium and want to have it, sure, you should get one. Later if you feel like you don't really need it because you wish to spend that time with family or friends, you can always return it. You can also decide to try a new gadget or a new hobby. The point is that a minimalist perspective offers a vibrant lifestyle. Security comes from being careful about what you wish for. Sometimes, less is more.

CONCLUSION

I want to express my heartfelt gratitude to each and every reader who has taken the chance to read my first book. Through the pages of this book, I have sought to convey my perspective on the pressing issue of climate change and offer potential solutions based on my personal experiences and learnings.

I understand that we may hold differing opinions, and I respect the diversity of thought. My intention in writing this book was to share my insights and initiate meaningful discussions on this important topic.

I hope that the ideas and insights shared within these pages have sparked new perspectives, provoked thought, and perhaps even inspired action.

I am grateful for your time and attention and thank you for being a part of this journey.

REFERENCES

1. https://unfccc.int/process-and-meetings/the-paris-agreement/the-paris-agreement
2. https://www.overshootday.org/about-Earth-overshoot-day/
3. https://www.carbonbrief.org/scientists-compare-climate-change-impacts-at-1-5c-and-2c/
4. https://www.americanchemistry.com/chemistry-in-america/chemistry-in-everyday-products/plastics
5. https://assets.publishing.service.gov.uk/government/uploads/system/uploads/attachment_data/file/291023/scho0711buan-e-e.pdf
6. https://allaboutbags.ca/
7. https://www2.mst.dk/Udgiv/publications/2018/02/978-87-93614-73-4.pdf
8. https://www.trvst.world/sustainable-living/eco-friendly/zero-waste-stores/
9. https://www.trvst.world/sustainable-living/eco-friendly/packaging/
10. https://www.conservation.org/blog/mcdonalds-to- take-a- bite-out-of-carbon-emissions
11. https://knowledge.insead.edu/ethics/measuring-the-green-label-1560
12. https://www.fao.org/india/fao-in-india/india-at-a-glance/en/#:~:text=Agriculture%2C%20with%20its%20allied%20sectors,275%20million%20tonnes%20(MT)
13. https://www.wbdg.org/resources/retrofitting-existing-buildings-improve-sustainability-and-energy-performance
14. https://www.theguardian.com/sustainable-business/retrofitting-older-buildings-innovations-necessity

15. https://publications.jrc.ec.europa.eu/repository/
16. https://www3.weforum.org/docs/WEF_System_Value_Europe_Market_Analysis_2020.pdf
17. https://www.wbdg.org/resources/moisture-management
18. https://www.wbdg.org/resources/energy-efficient-lighting
19. https://www.wbdg.org/resources/natural-ventilation
20. https://www.wbdg.org/ffc/doe/criteria/guide-integrating-renewable-energy-federal-construction
21. https://www.wbdg.org/resources/windows-and- glazing
22. https://www.wbdg.org/resources/distributed-energy-resources-der
23. https://www.wbdg.org/resources/extensive- vegetative-roofs
24. https://www.wbdg.org/design-objectives/sustainable
25. https://www.wbdg.org/design-objectives/sustainable/optimize-operational-maintenance-practices
26. https://www.wbdg.org/resources/measuring-performance-sustainable-buildings
27. https://www.thehindu.com/life-and-style/homes-and-gardens/organo-naandi-hyderabad-telangana-rurban-eco- living/article33994262.ece
28. https://www.thecatskillproject.com/homes/

ABOUT THE AUTHOR

Niharika Kosanam is the Founder of Continuum Studio, a firm that strives to achieve sustainability in every aspect of living. Niharika is a LEED Accredited Professional and IGBC Accredited professional who carries end-to-end practical knowledge in Building Design, Construction Management, Business Development, and Sustainable Design. Her aim is to make energy-efficient, green buildings that go beyond the certification norms of the modern construction industry through Sustainable Design, Value Engineering, and Green Principles. Niharika hopes to bring real value through awareness and practical training programs to developers and corporations beyond rendering green consulting services.